# HALLOWEEN PARTY

## MONSTER COLORING BOOK





MICHAEL LOZANO AND DAVID PEREZ



SOUTH FLORIDA
BOOKS

Halloween Party

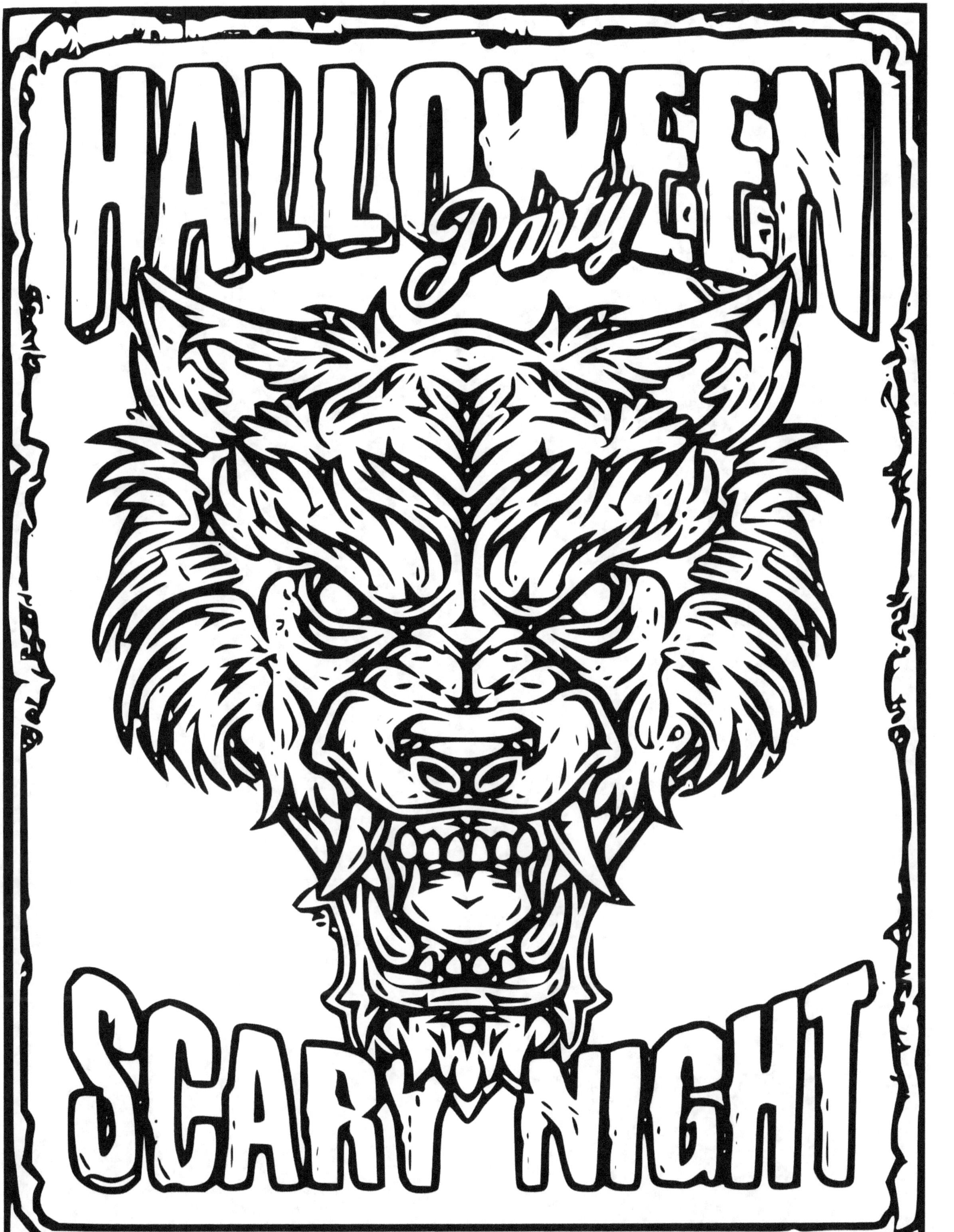
HALLOWEEN
Party
SCARY NIGHT

Halloween Party

HALLOWEEN
Party
Hunting
SCARY NIGHT

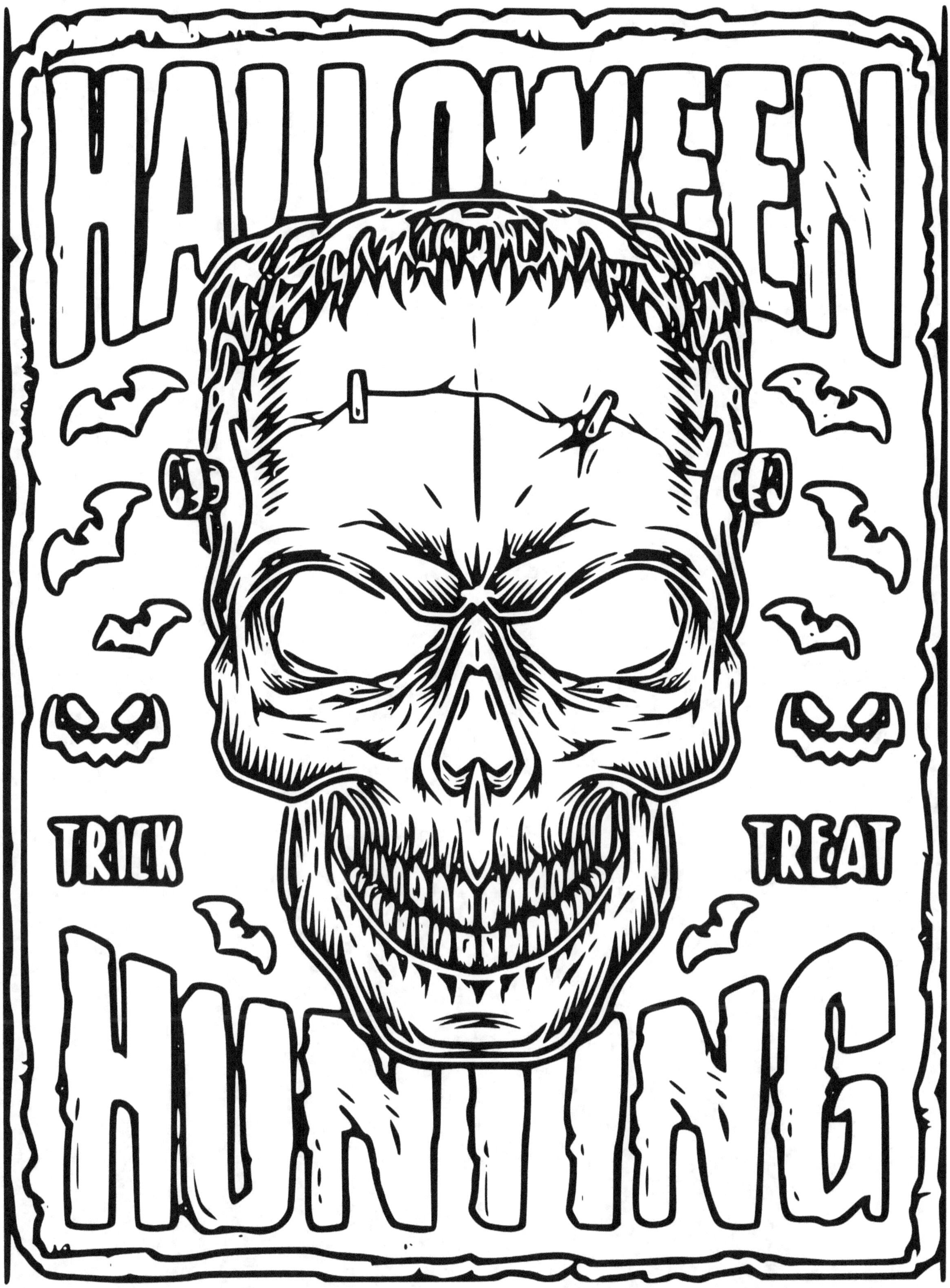
HALLOWEEN
TRICK
TREAT
HUNTING

Halloween Party

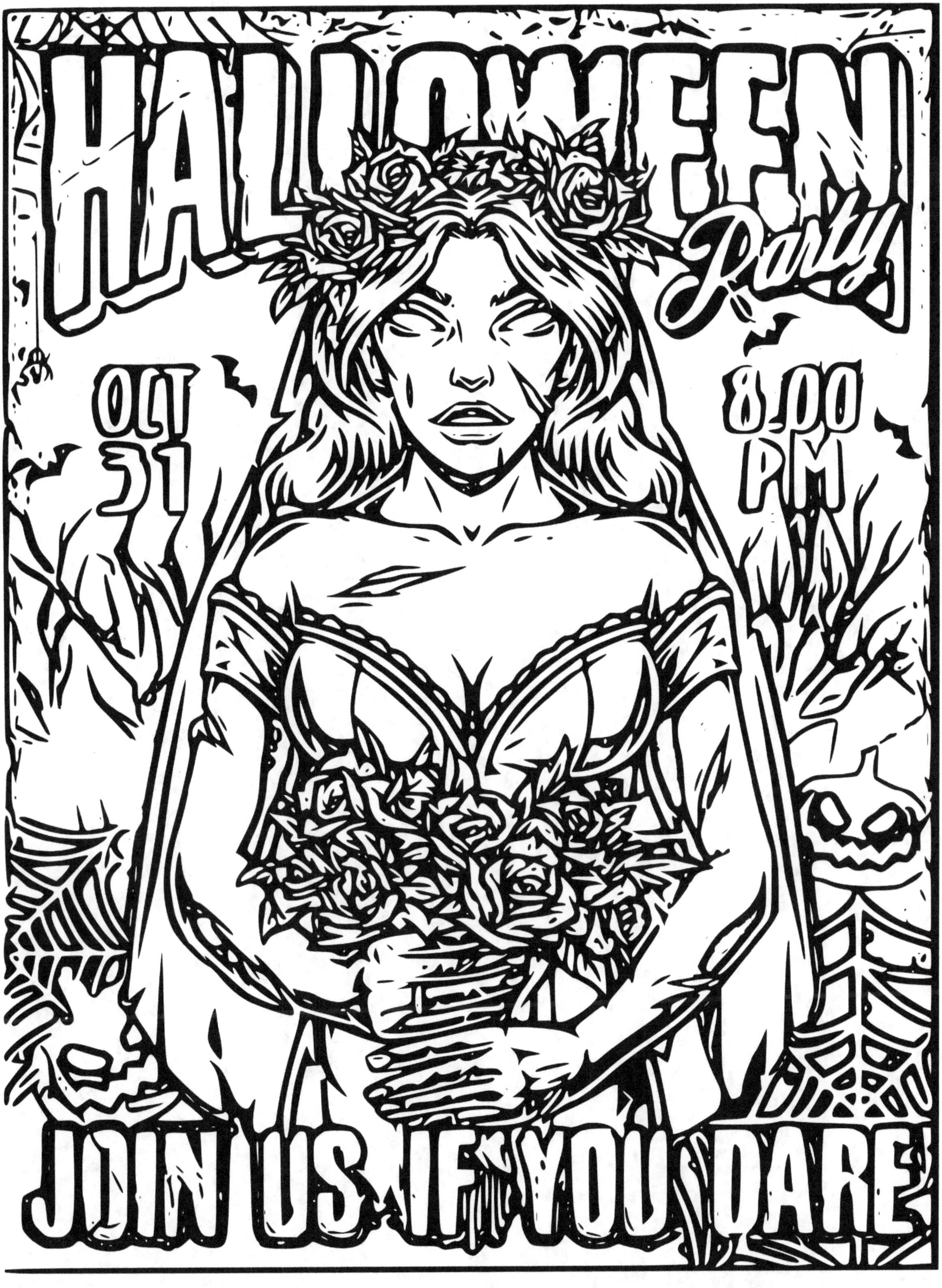
HALLOWEEN
Party
OCT
31
8.00
PM
JOIN US IF YOU DARE!

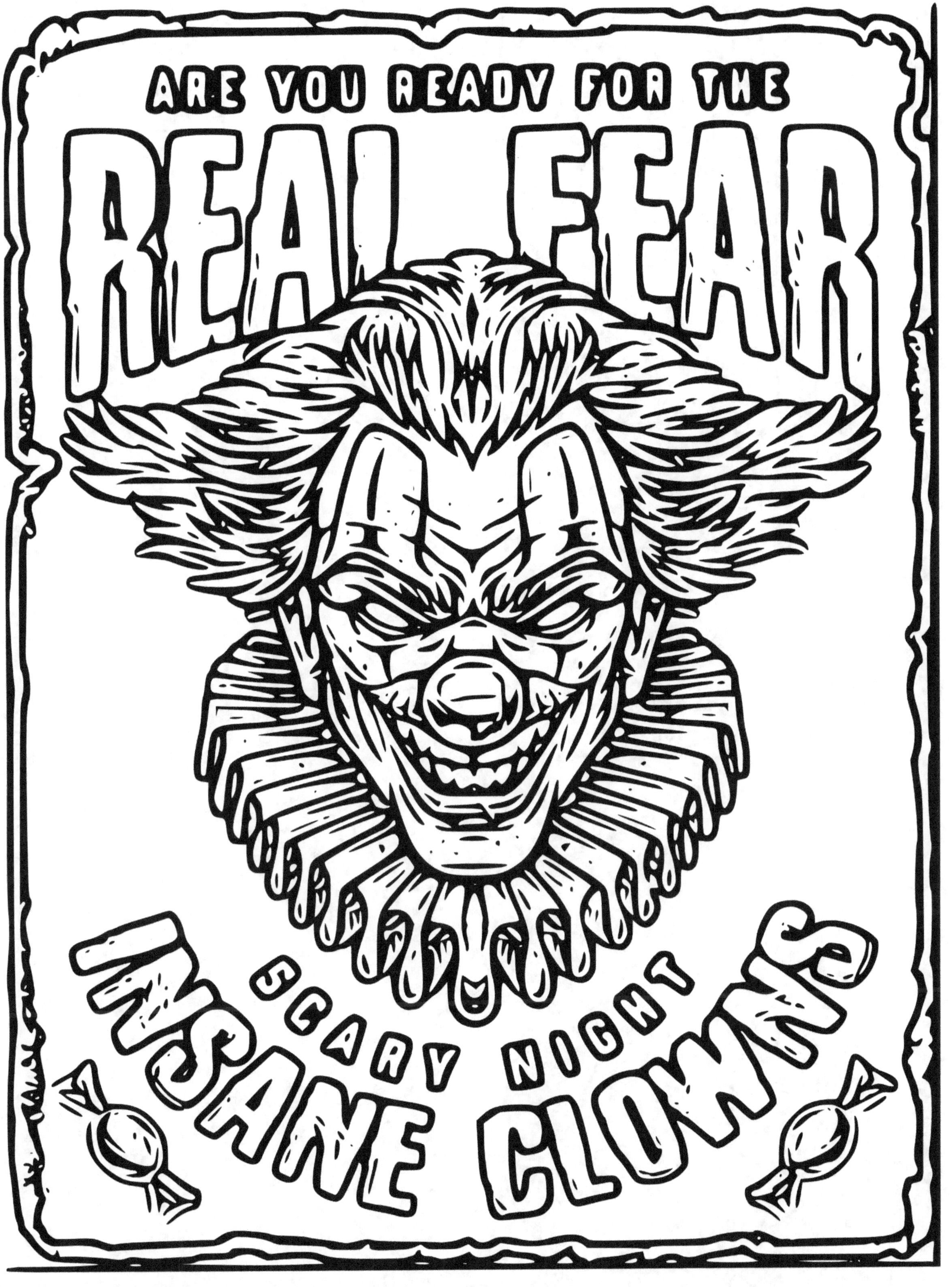
ARE YOU READY FOR THE
REAL FEAR
SCARY NIGHT
INSANE CLOWNS

Halloween Party

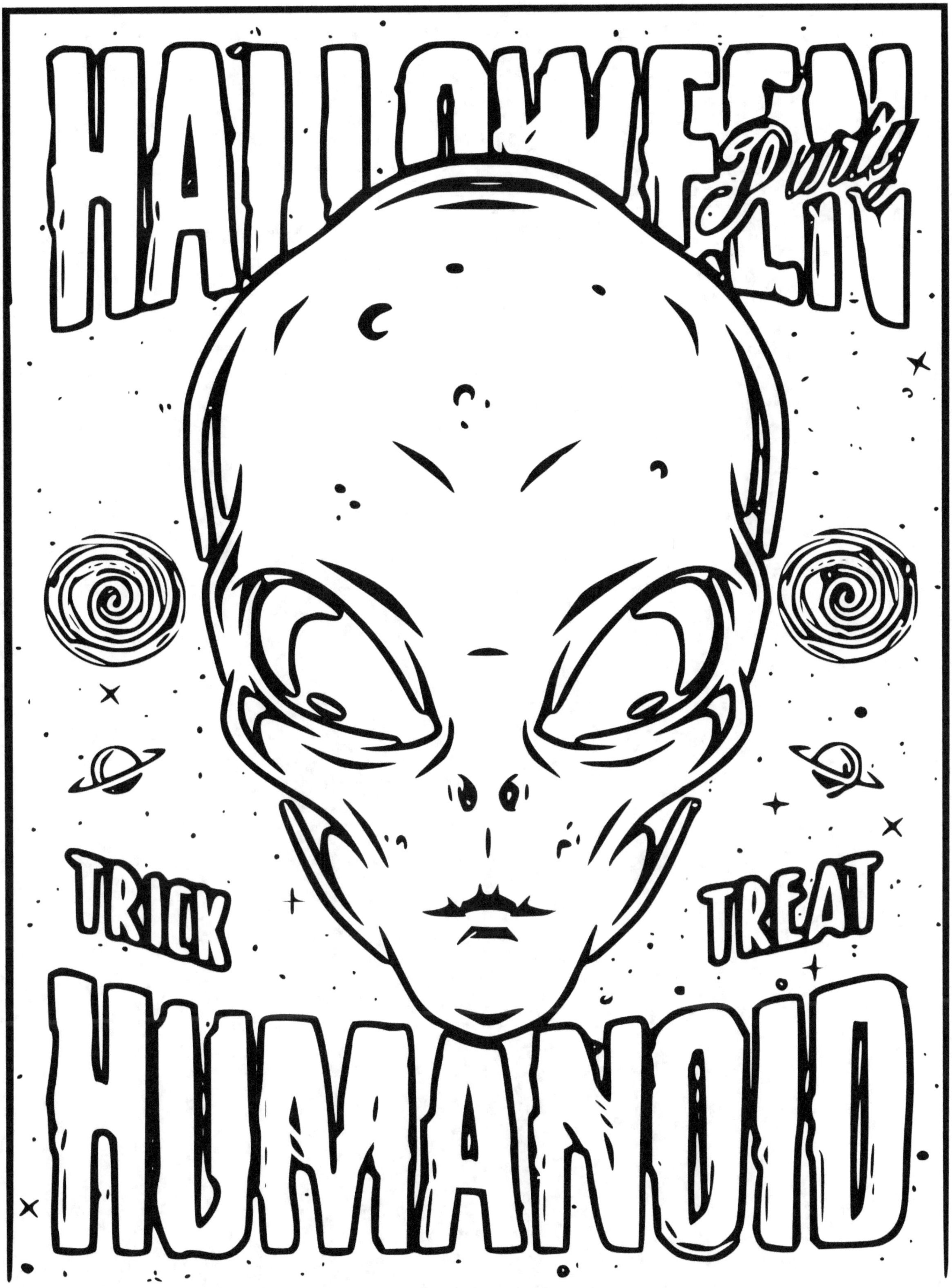
HALLOWEEN
Party
TRICK
TREAT
HUMANOID

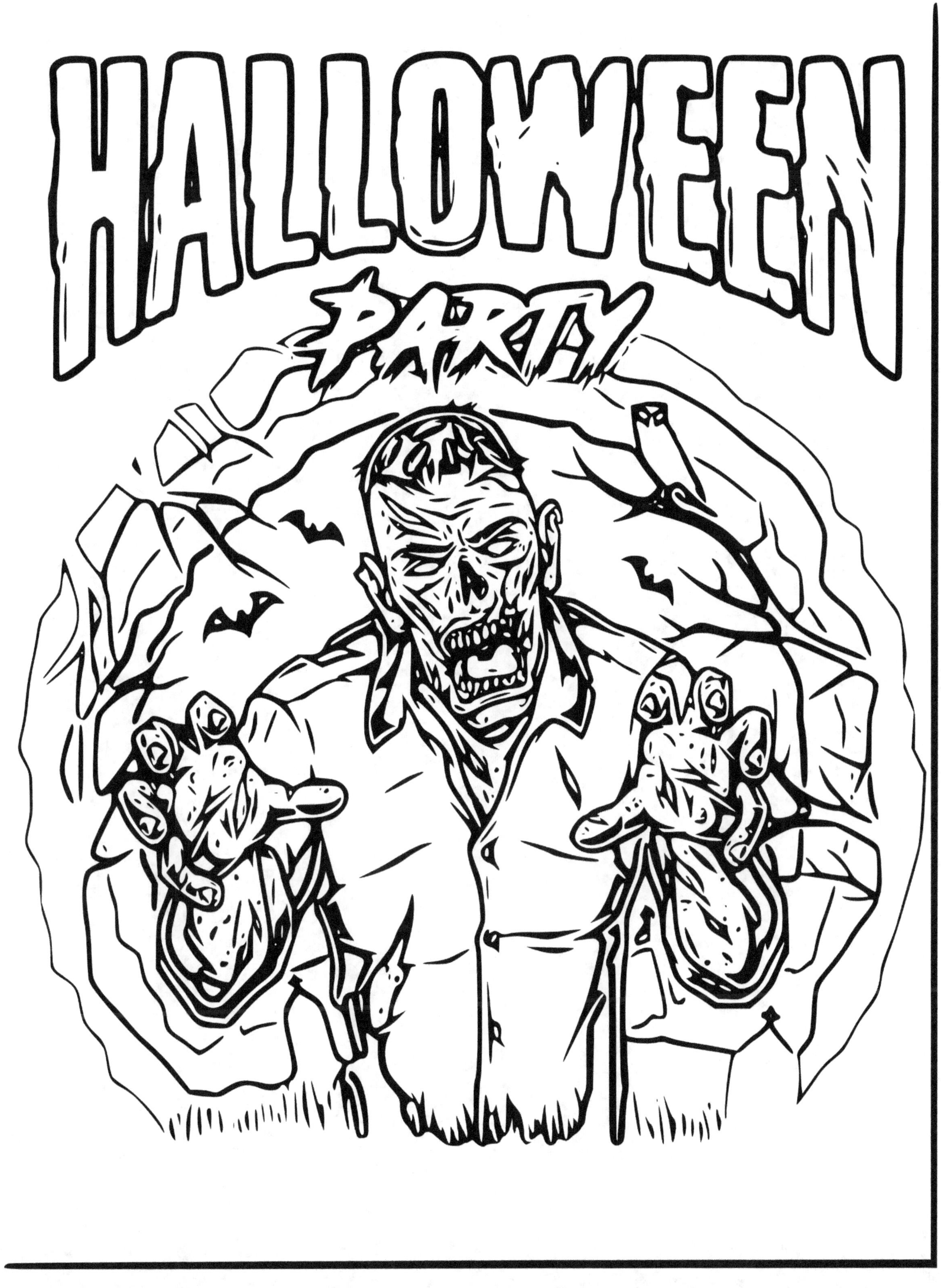
HALLOWEEN
PARTY

Halloween Party

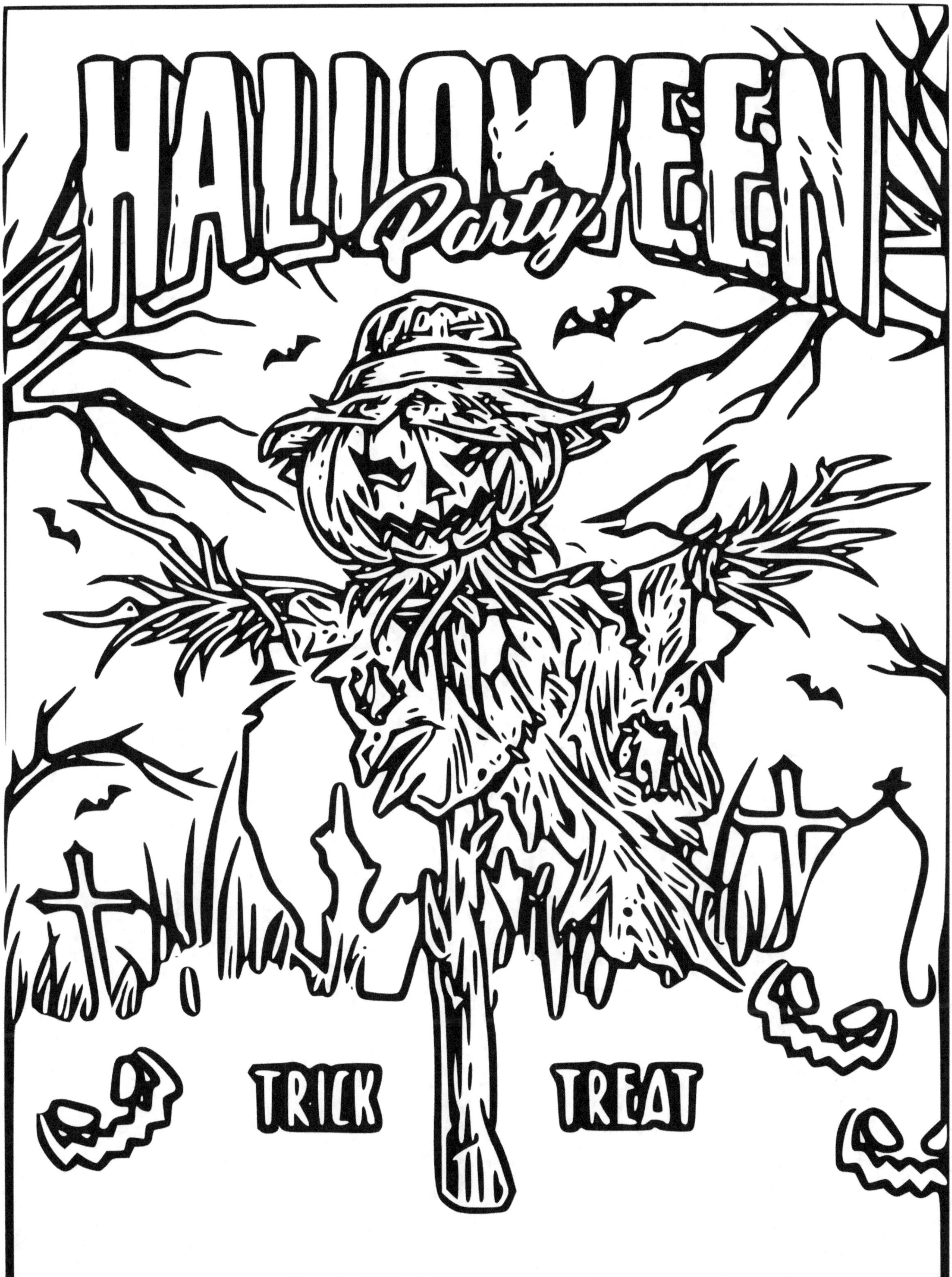
HALLOWEEN
Party
TRICK
TREAT

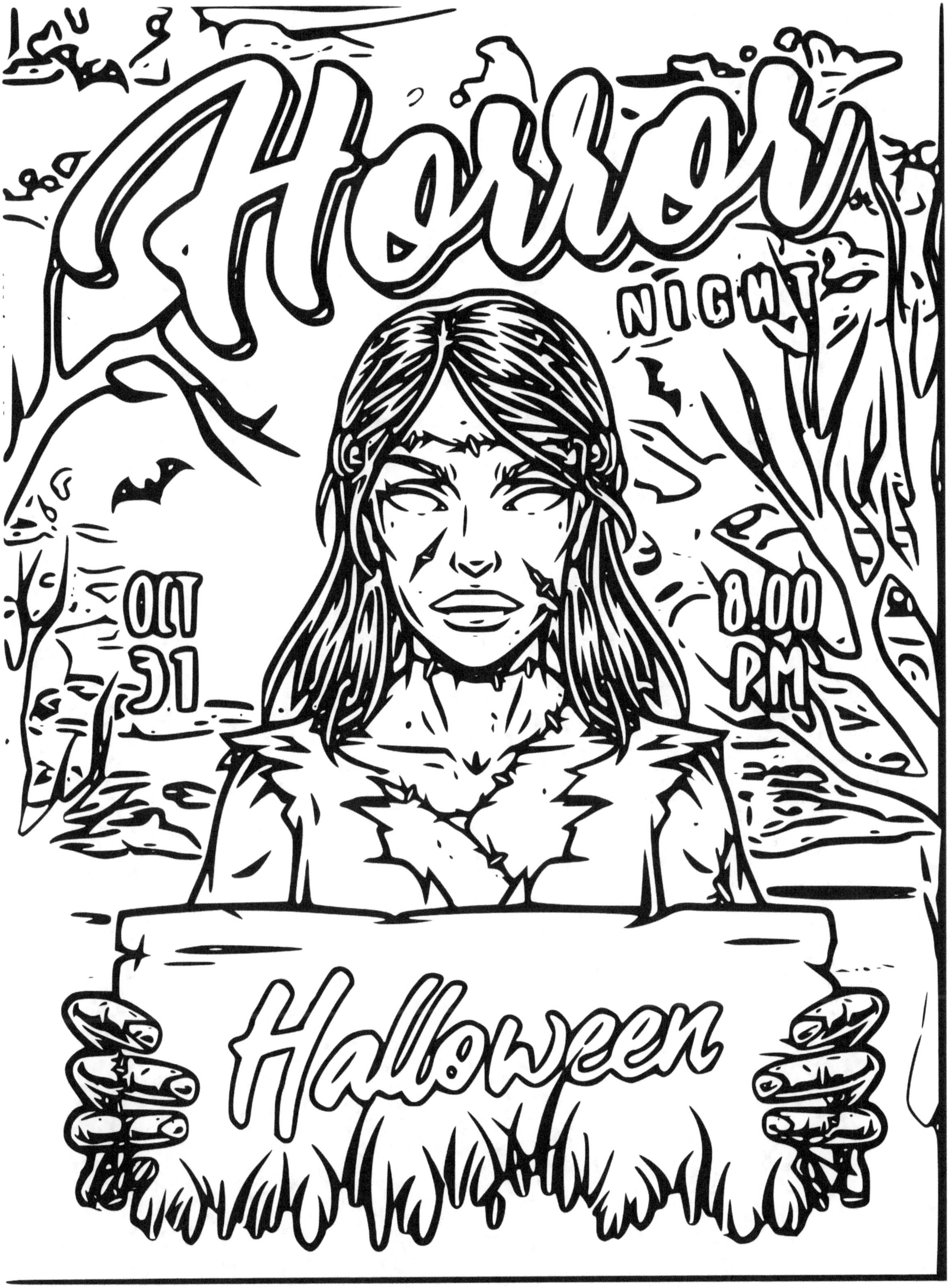
Horror
NIGHT
OCT
31
8.00
PM
Halloween

Halloween Party

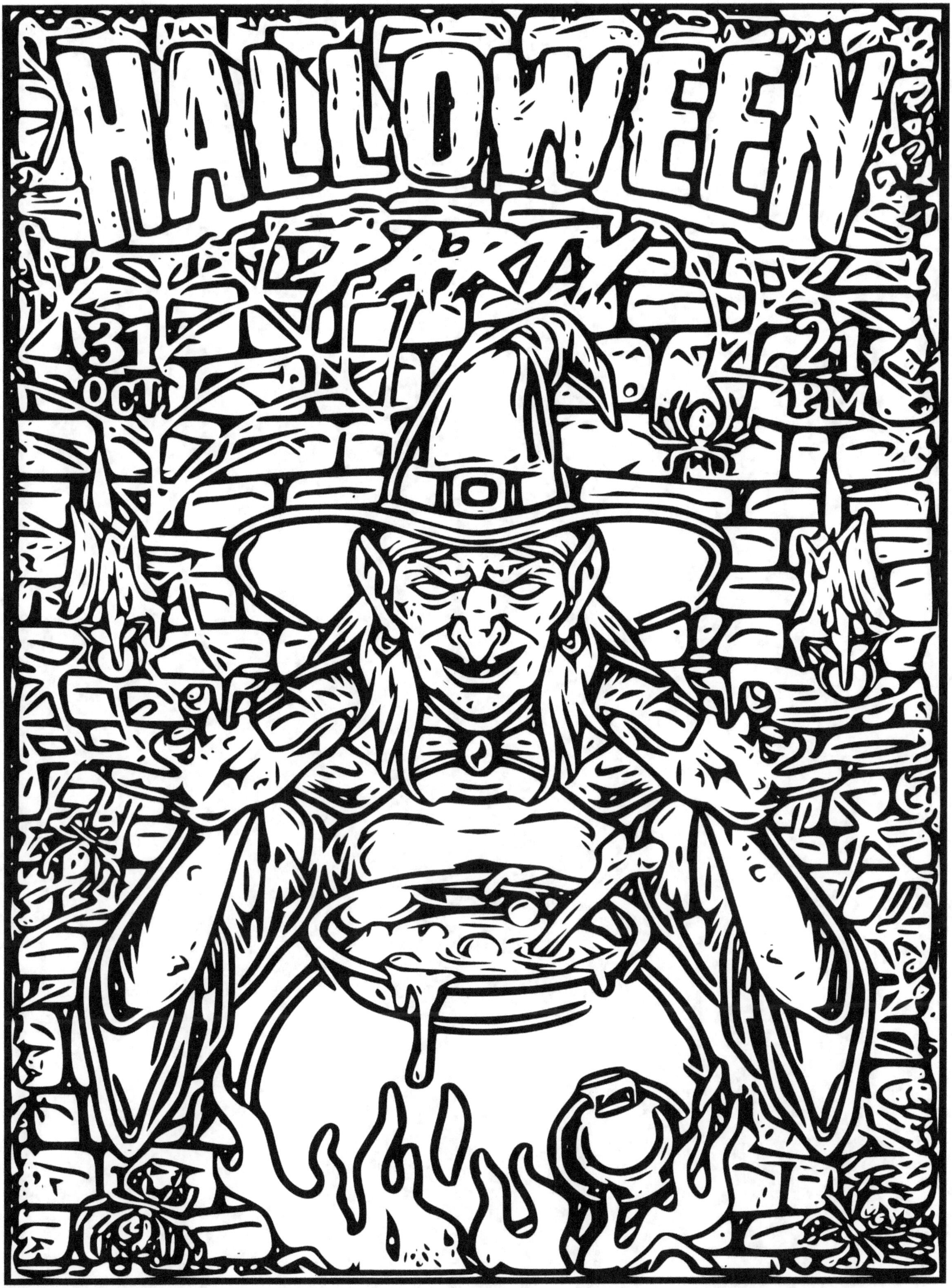
HALLOWEEN
PARTY
31
OCT
21
PM

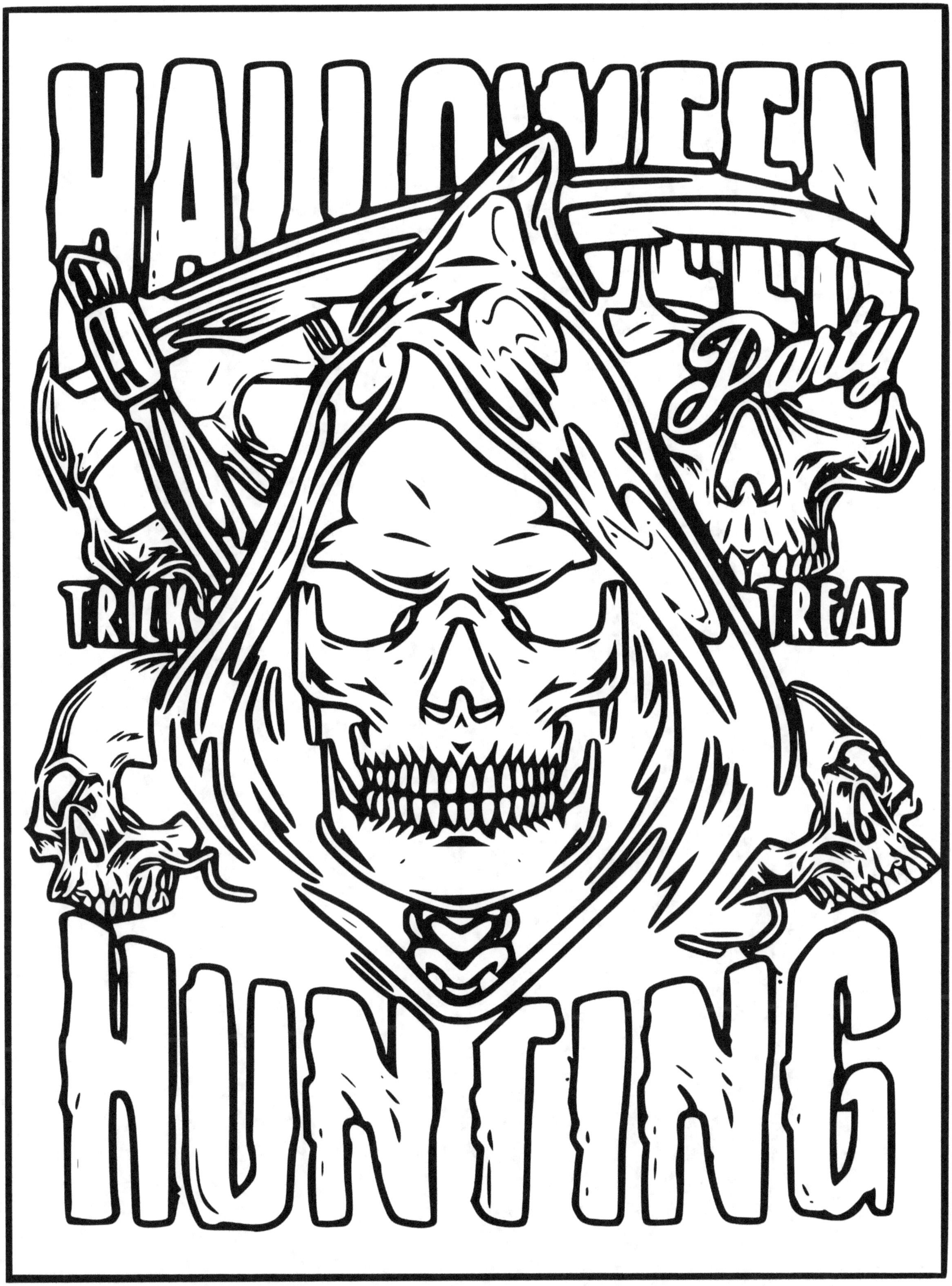

HALLOWEEN
Party
TRICK
TREAT
HUNTING

Halloween Party

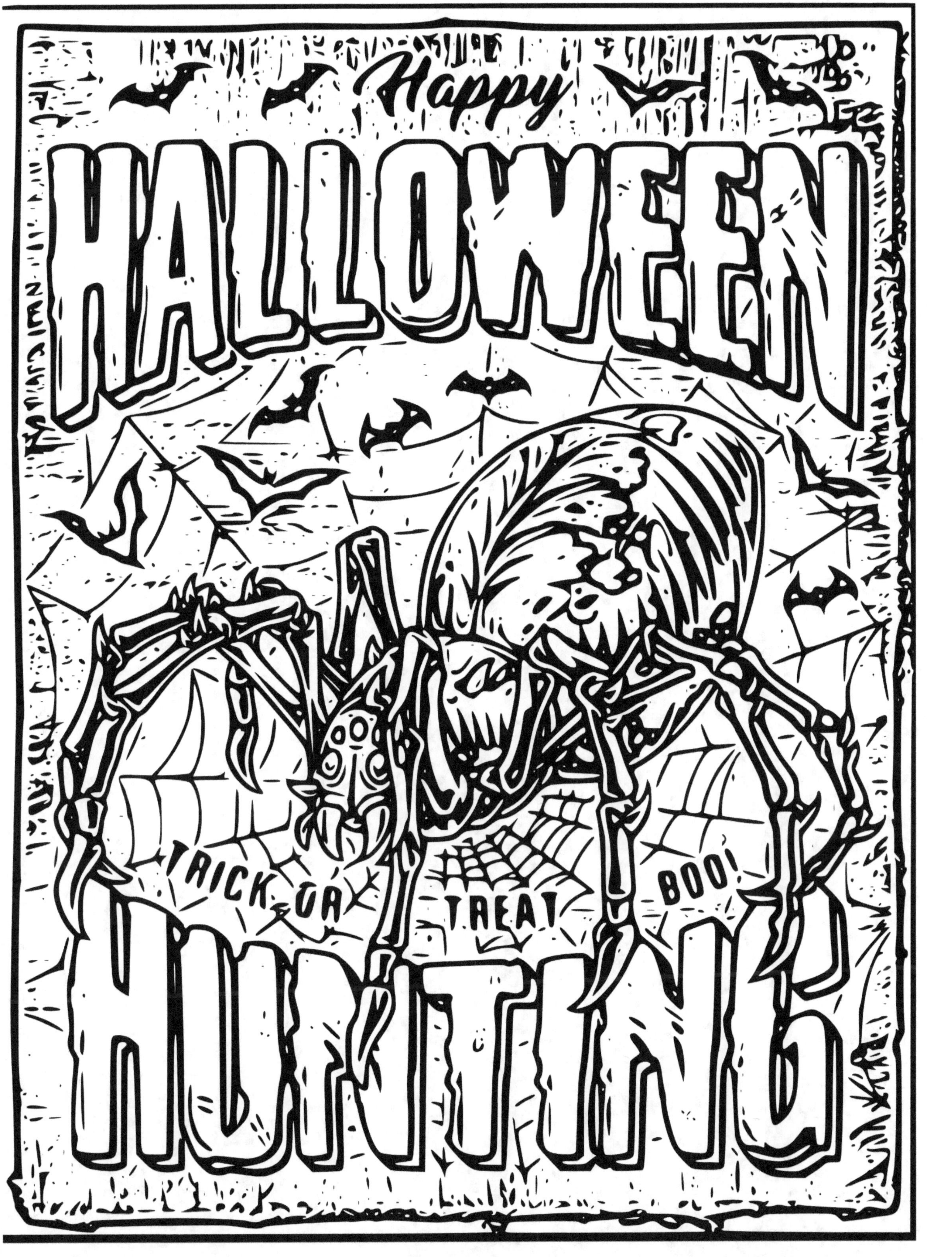
Happy
HALLOWEEN
TRICK OR
TREAT
BOO!
HUNTING

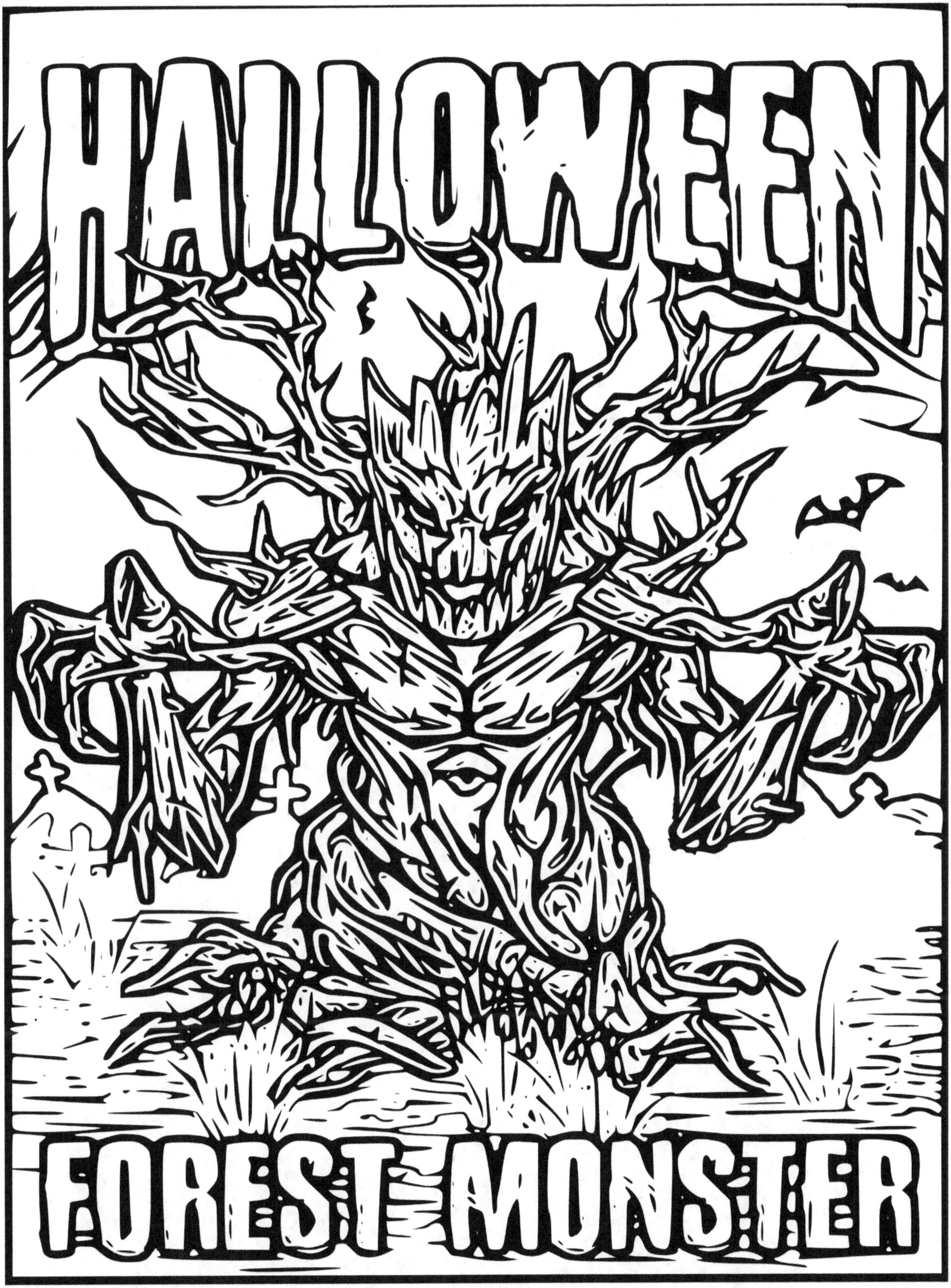
HALLOWEEN
FOREST MONSTER

Halloween Party

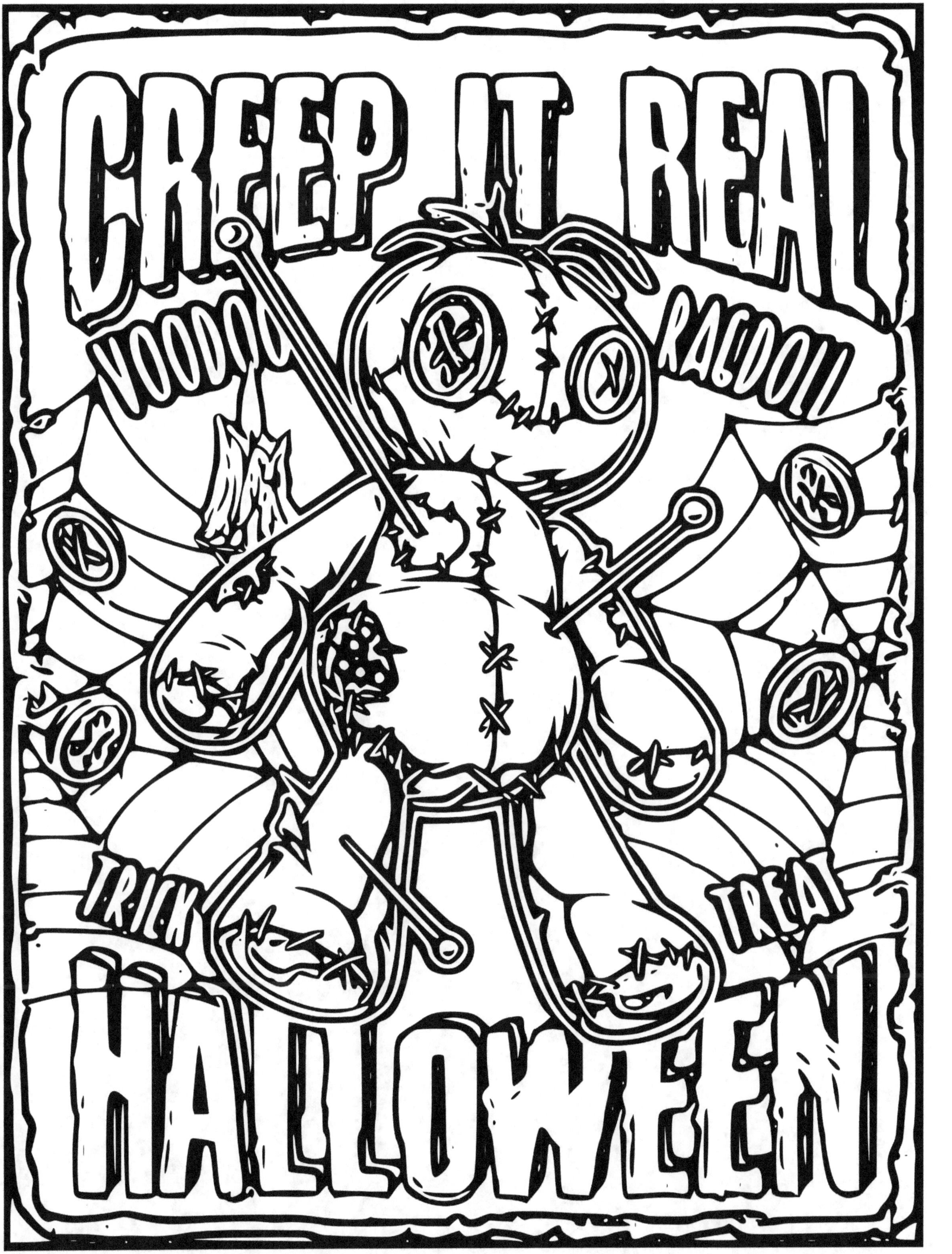
CREEP IT REAL
VOODOO
RAGDOLL
TRICK
TREAT
HALLOWEEN

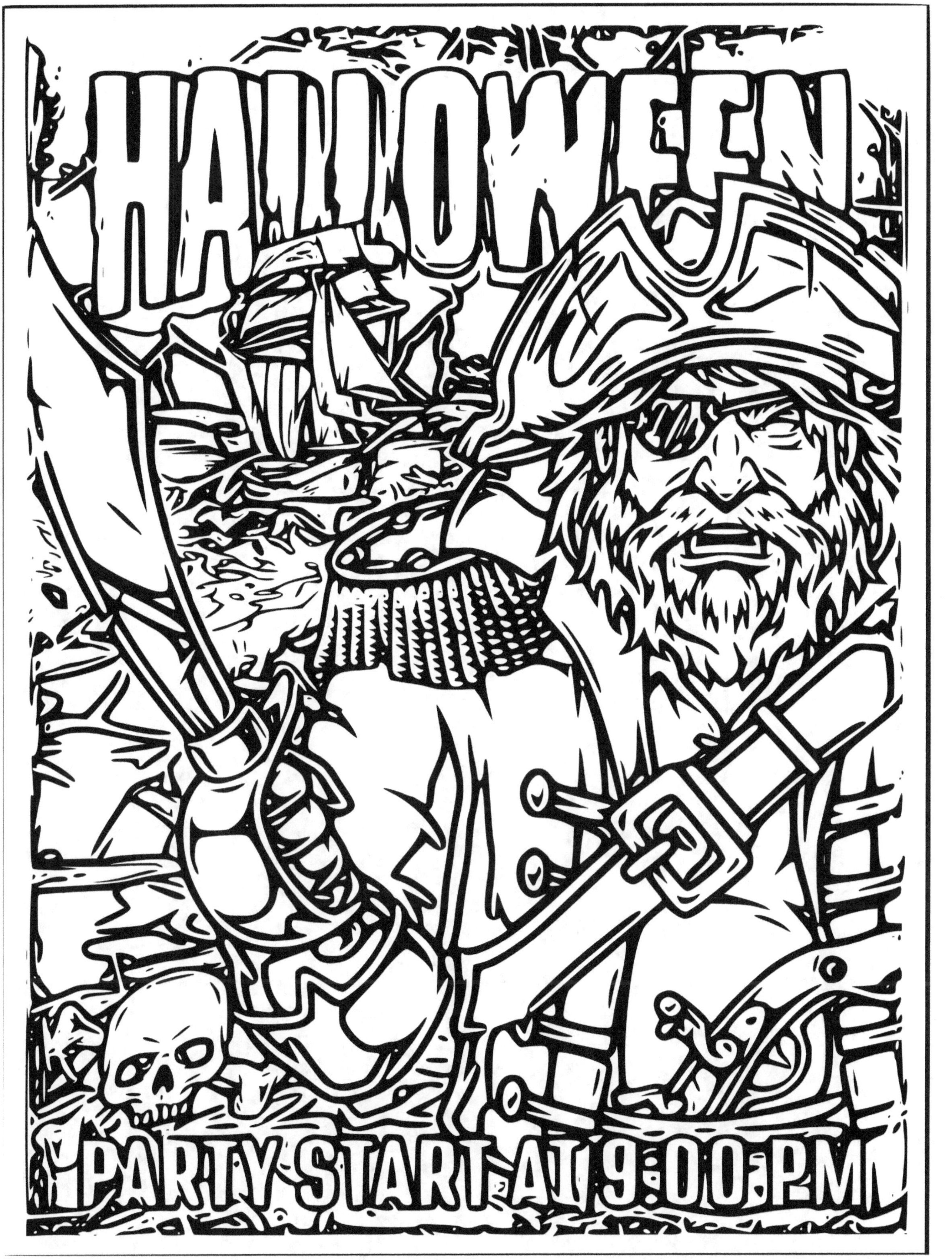
HALLOWEEN
PARTY START AT 9:00 PM

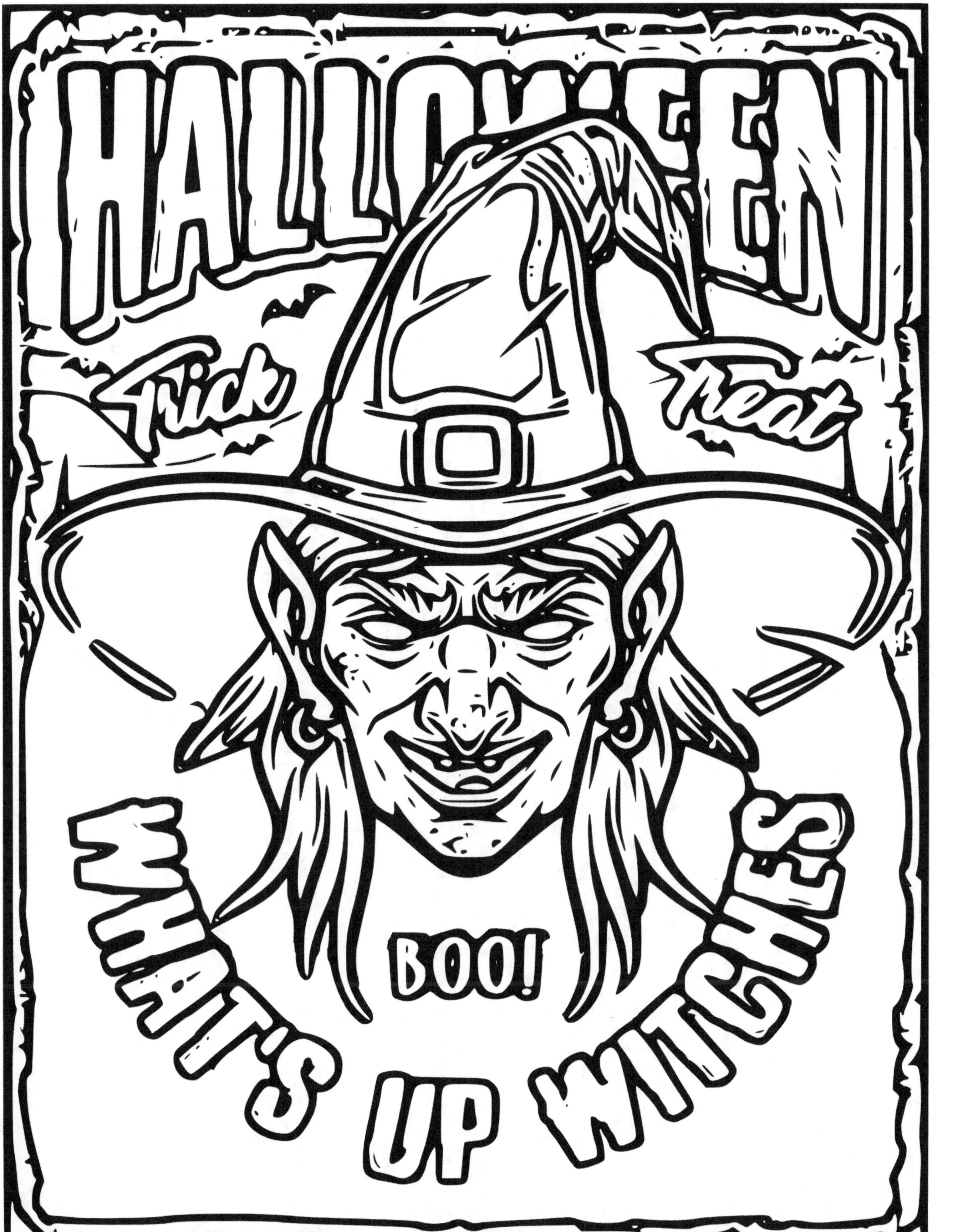
HALLOWEEN
Trick
Treat
BOO!
WHAT'S UP WITCHES

HALLOWEEN
PARTY
31 OCT.
21 PM...
Trick or Treat

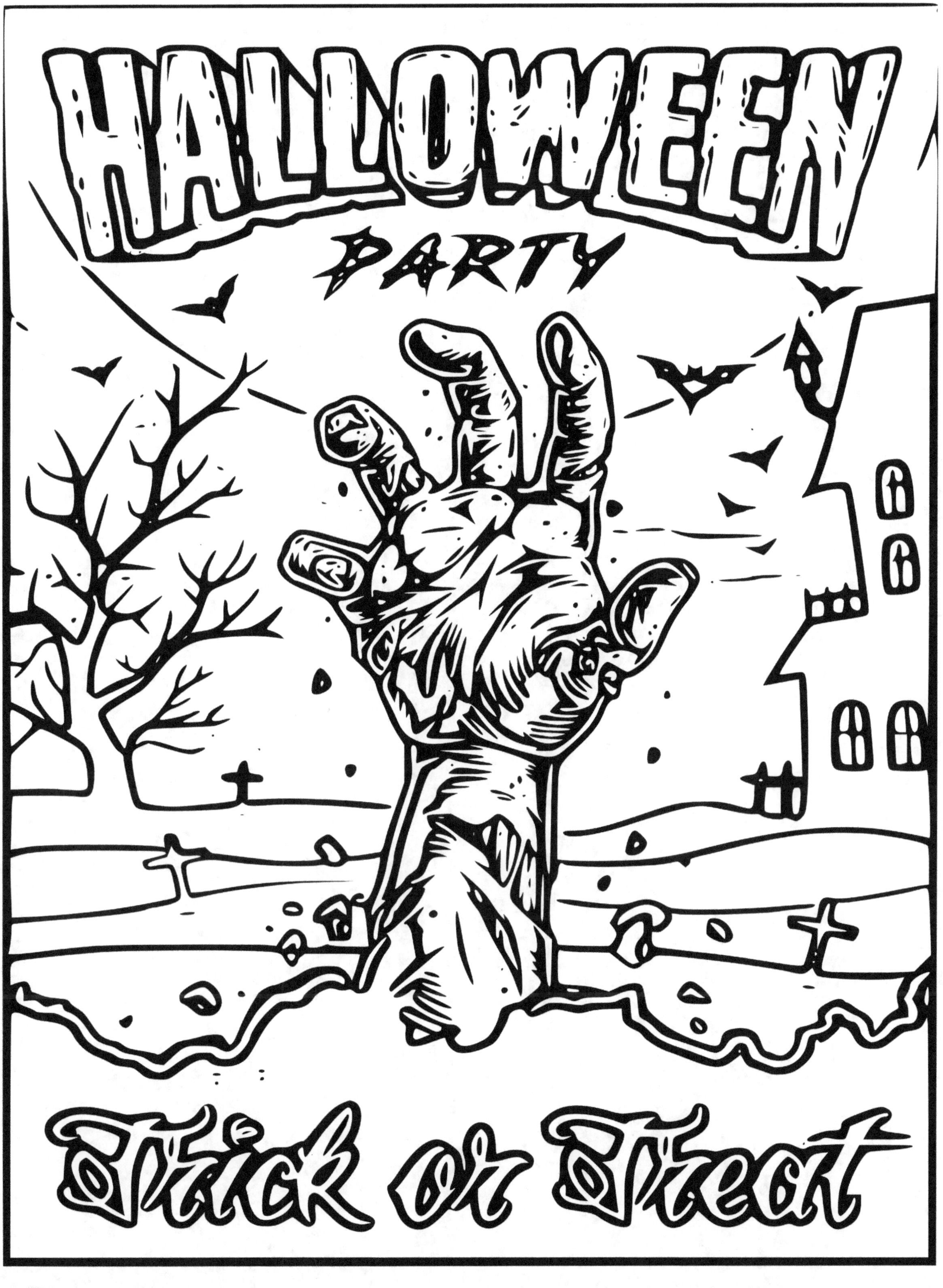
HALLOWEEN
PARTY
Trick or Treat

Halloween Party

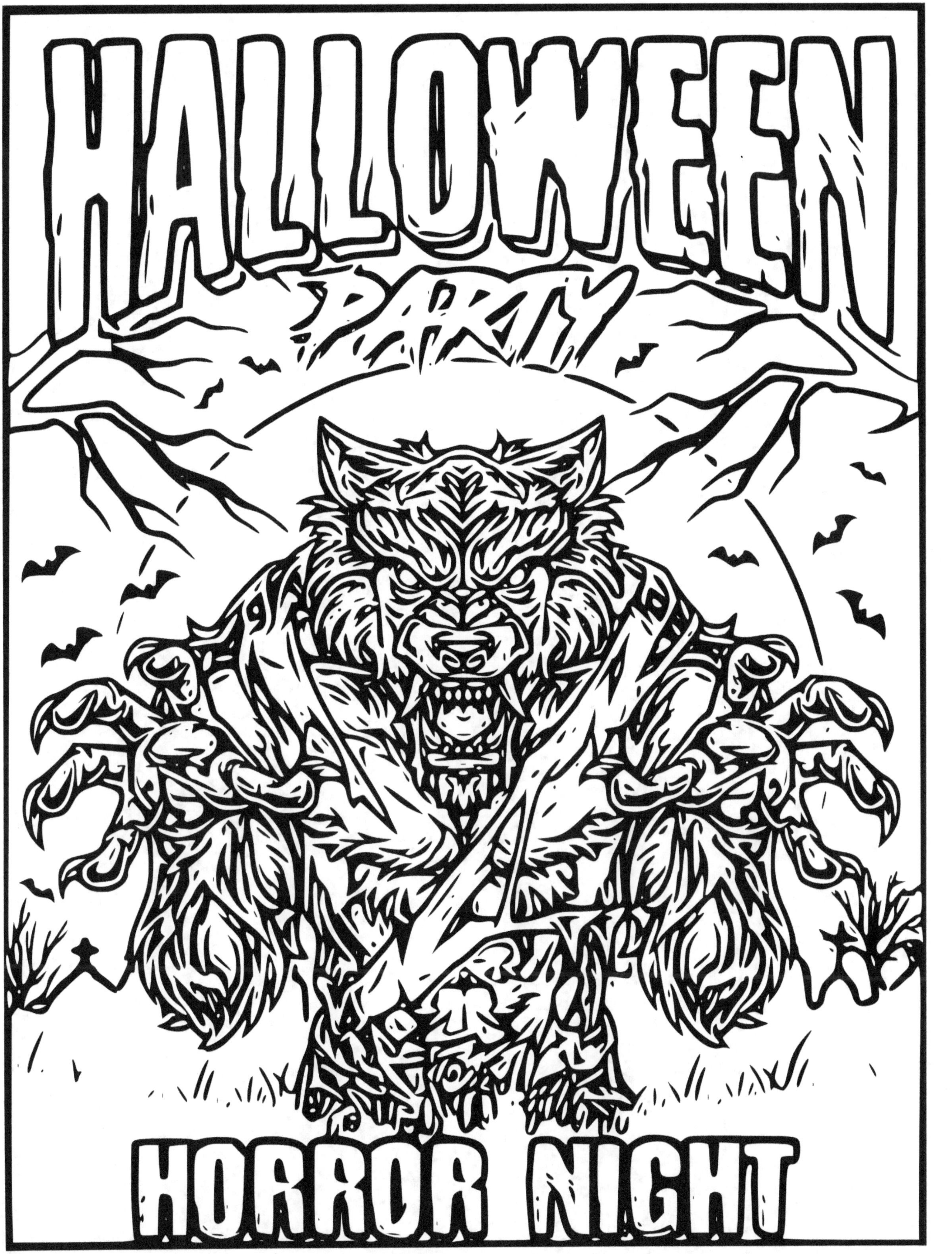
HALLOWEEN
PARTY
HORROR NIGHT

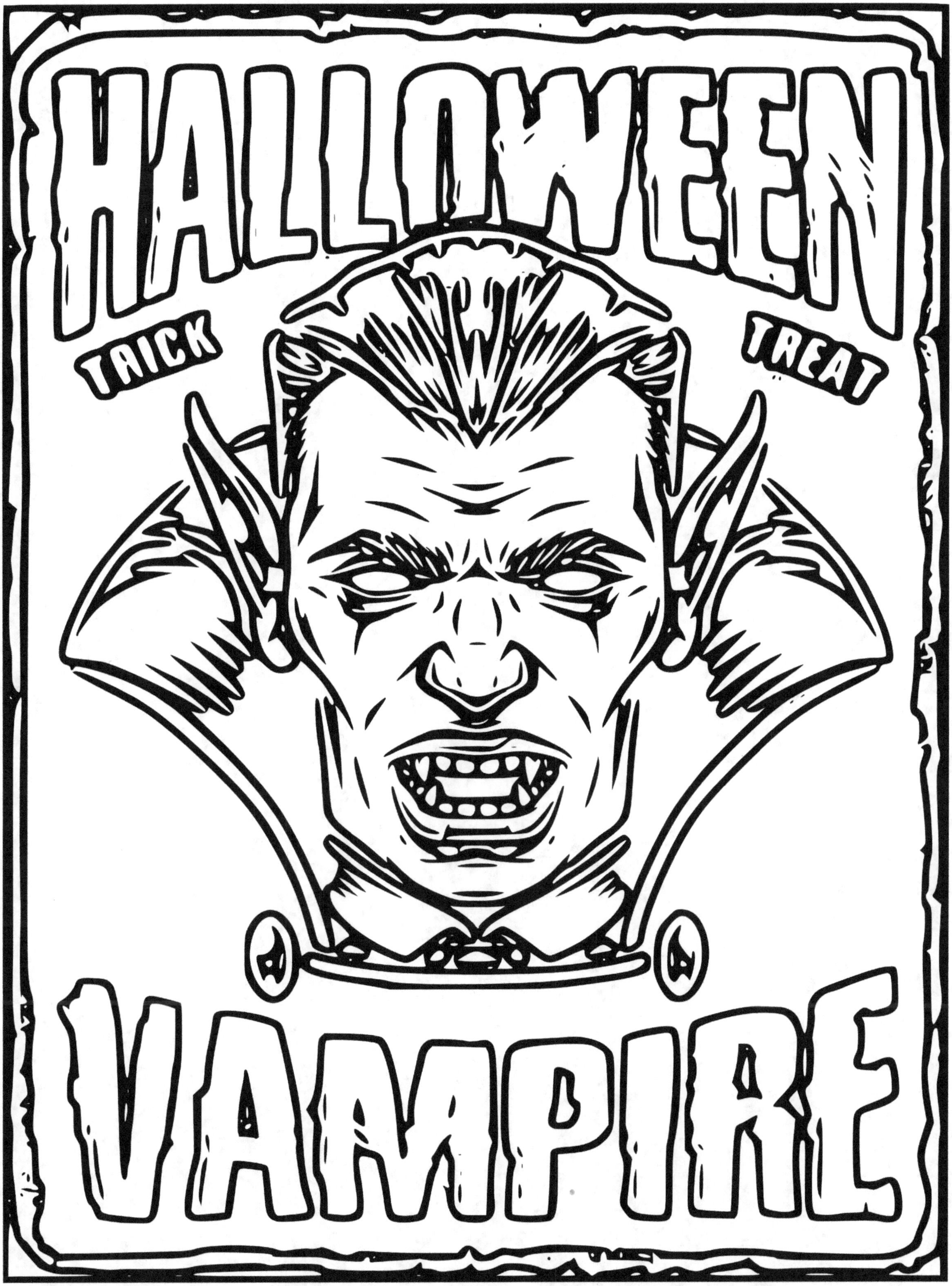
HALLOWEEN
TRICK
TREAT
VAMPIRE

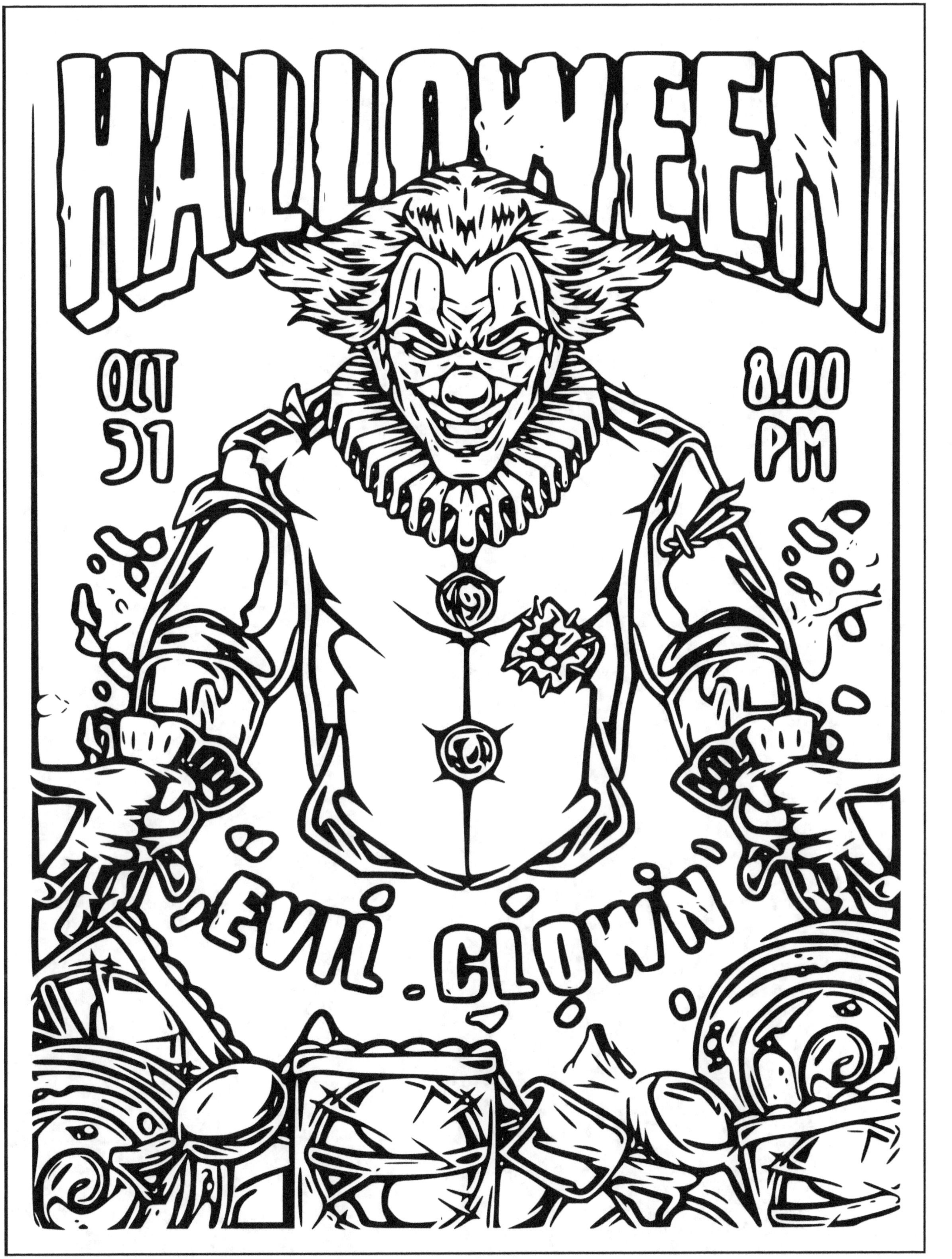
HALLOWEEN
OCT
31
8.00
PM
EVIL CLOWN

Halloween Party

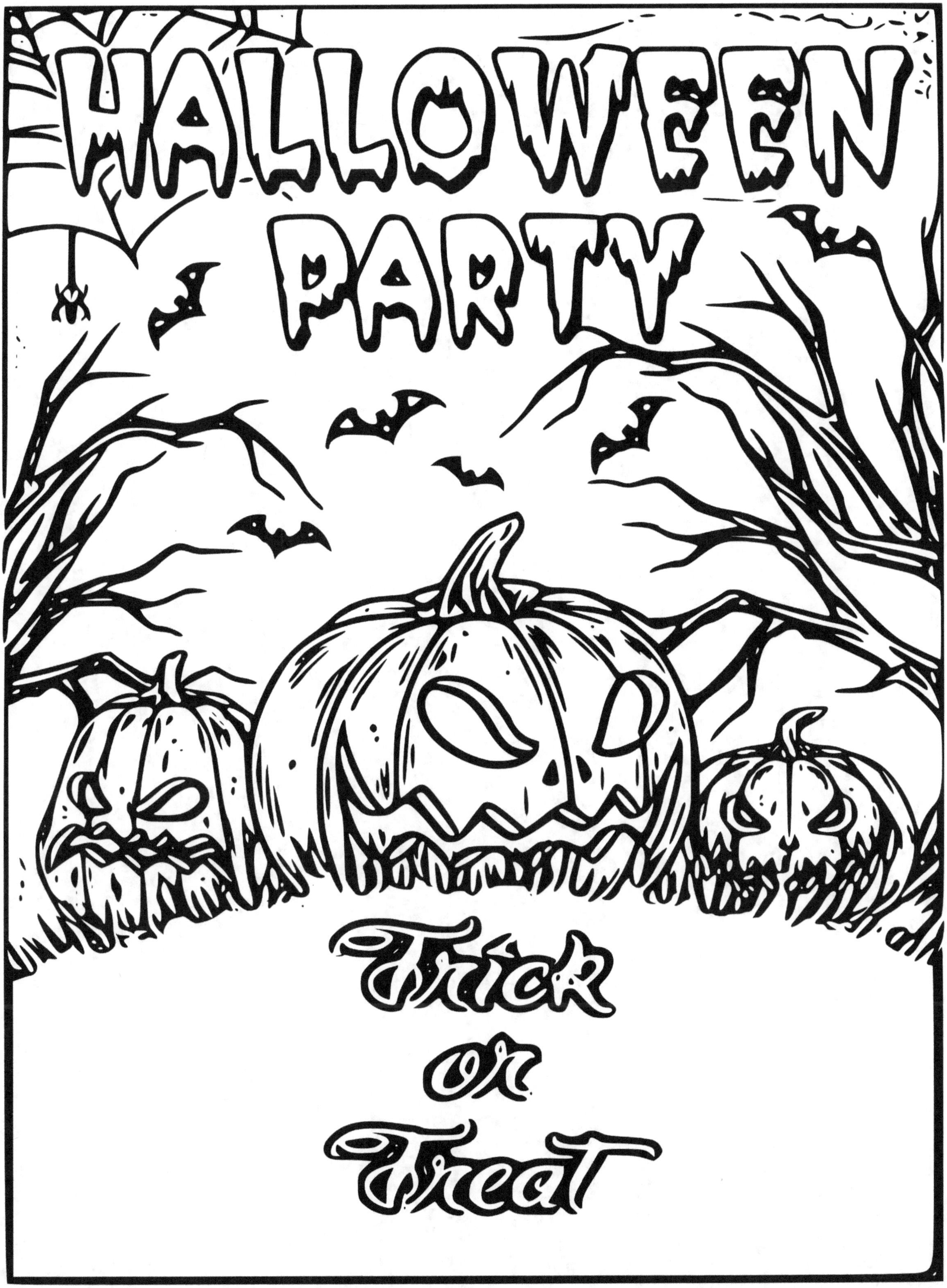
HALLOWEEN
PARTY
Trick
or
Treat

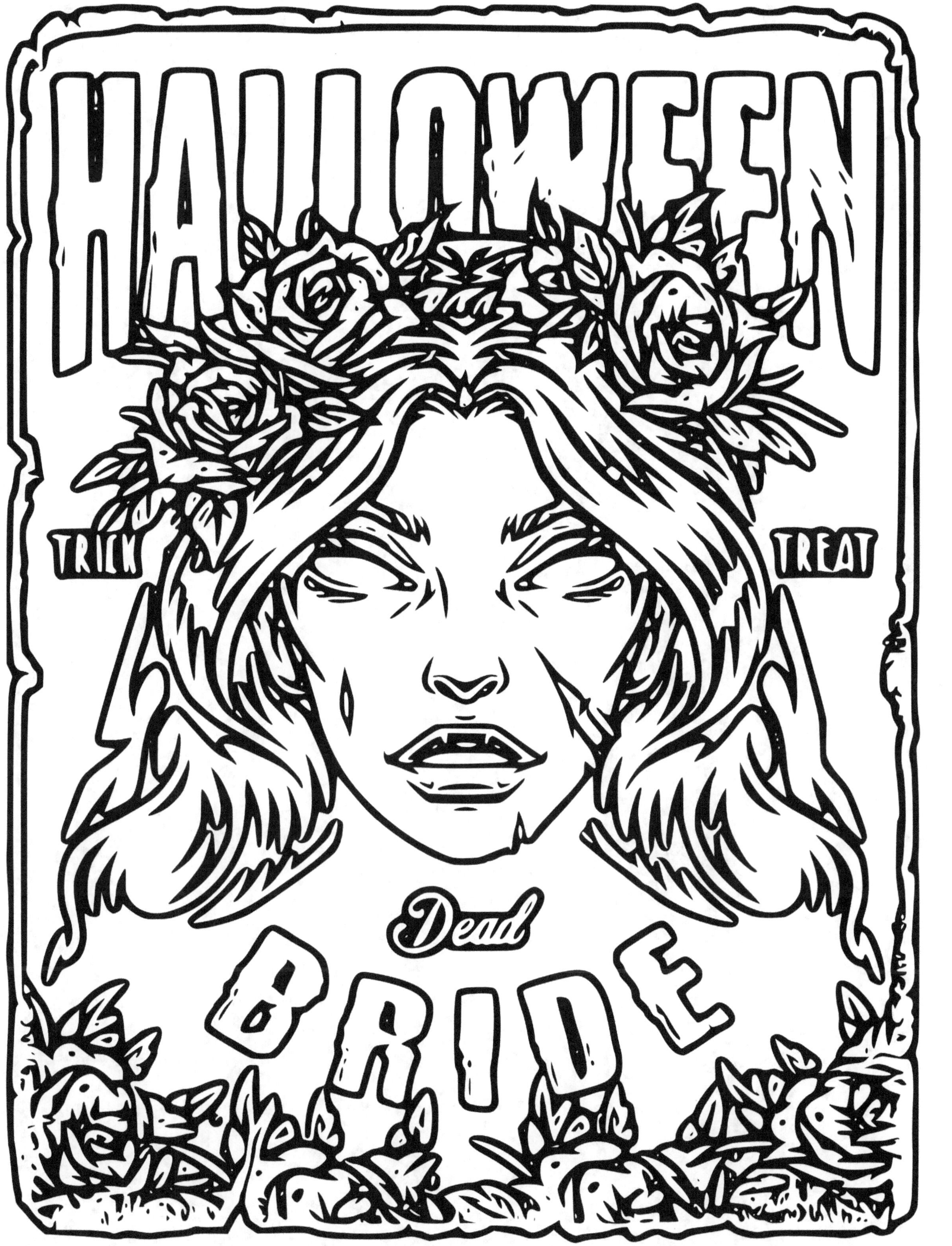
HALLOWEEN
TRICK
TREAT
Dead
BRIDE

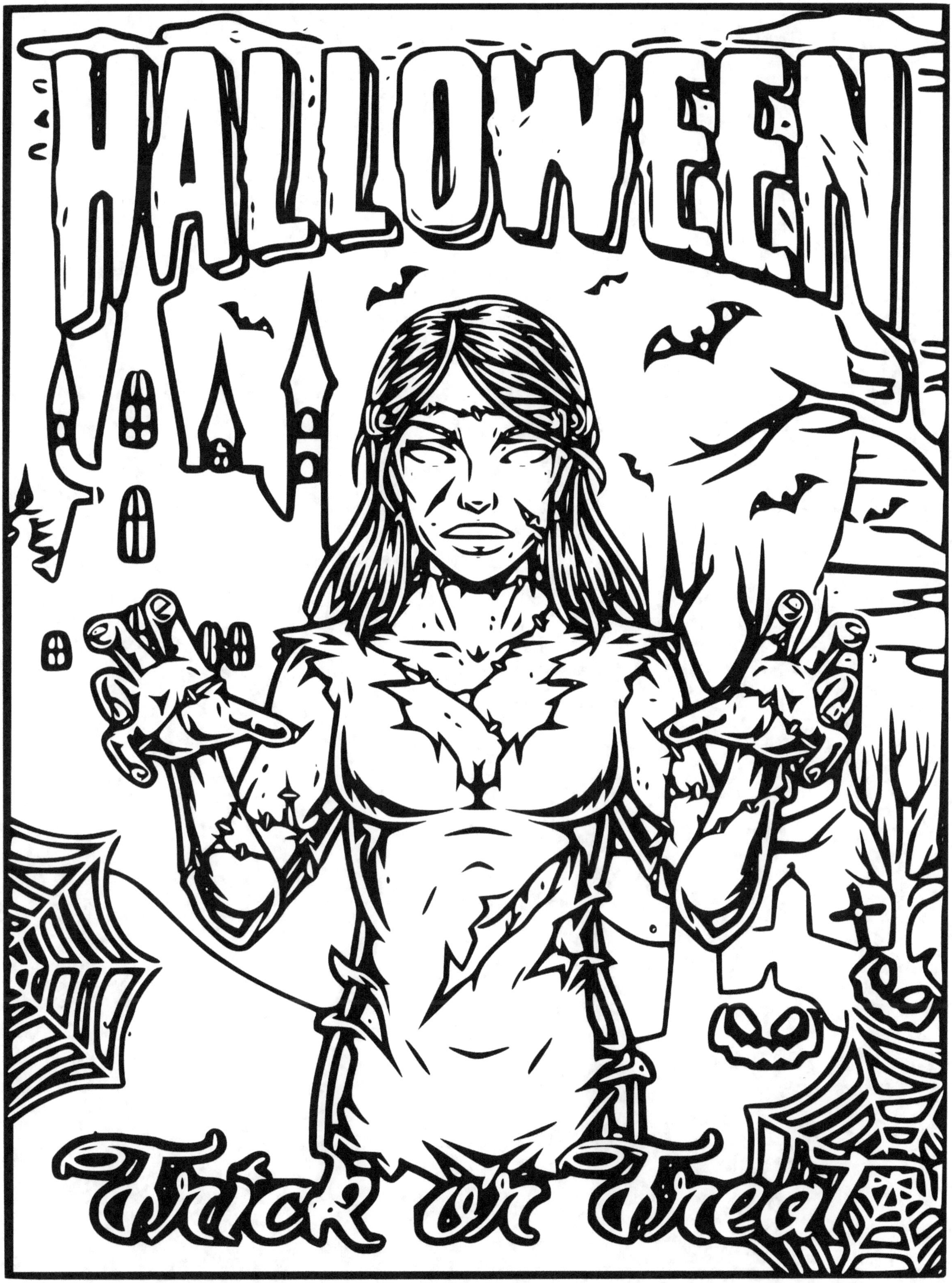
HALLOWEEN
Trick or Treat

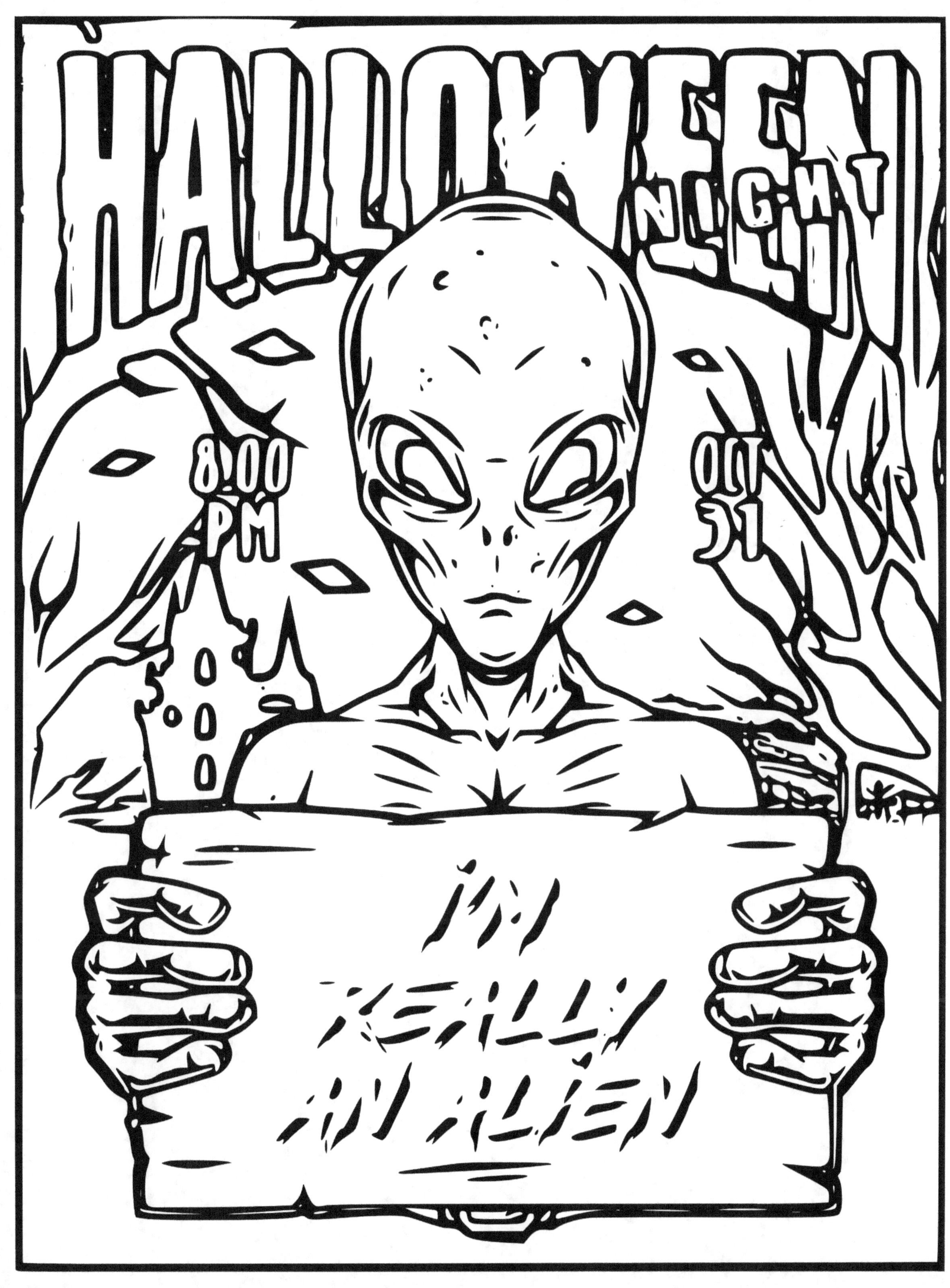
HALLOWEEN
NIGHT
8:00 PM
OCT 31
I'M
REALLY
AN ALIEN

Halloween Party

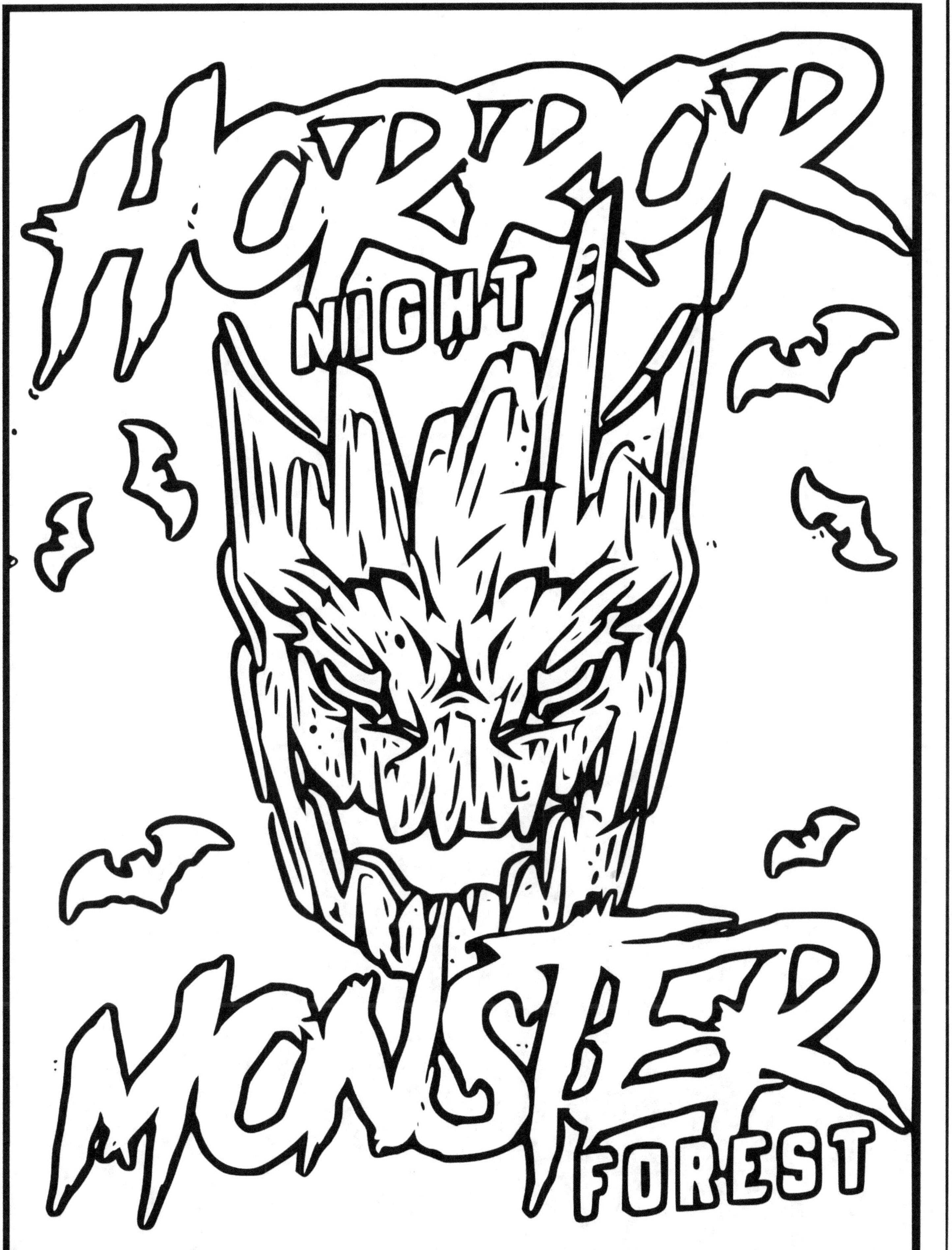
HORROR
NIGHT
MONSTER
FOREST

Halloween Party

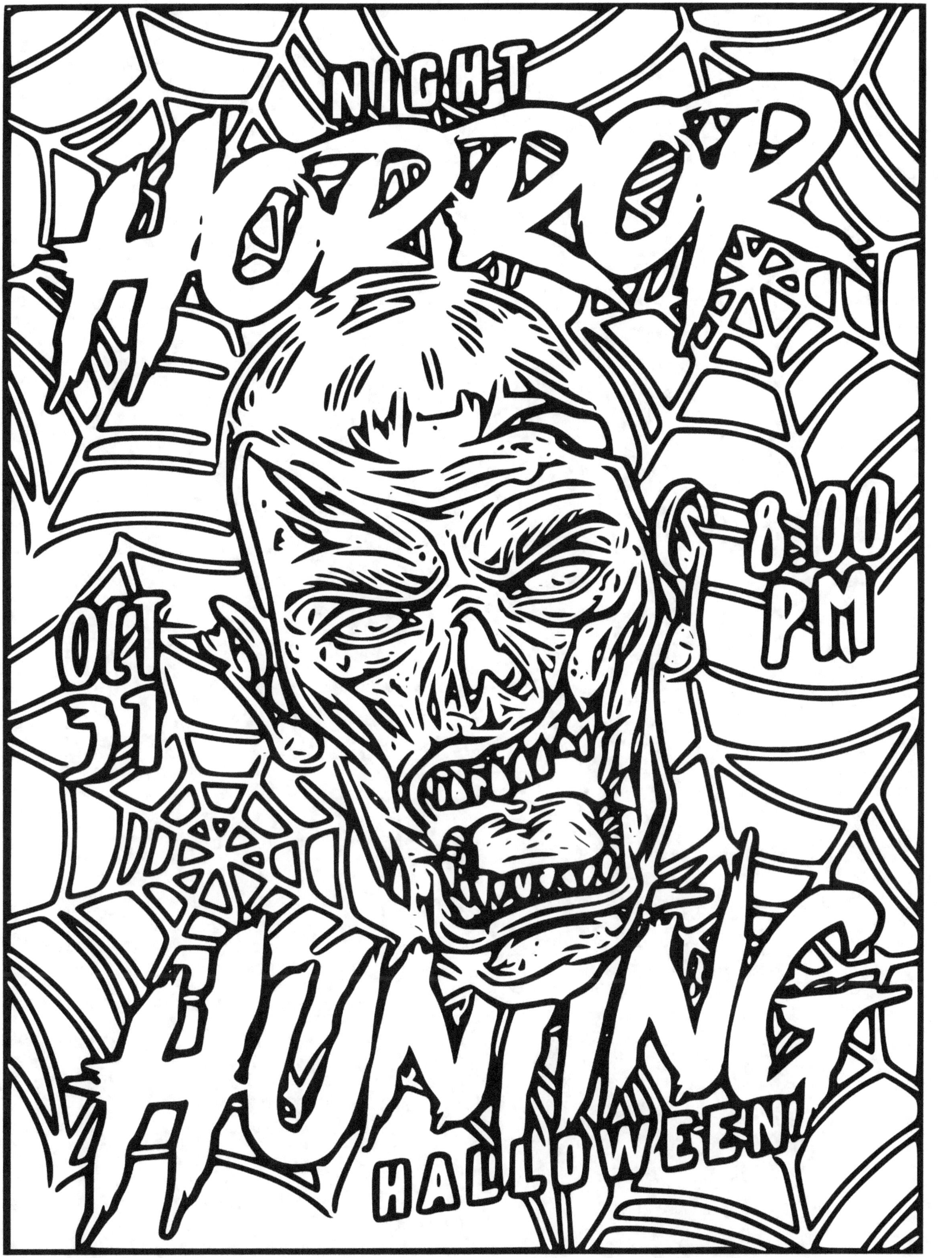
NIGHT
HORROR
8:00
PM
OCT
31
HUNTING
HALLOWEEN!

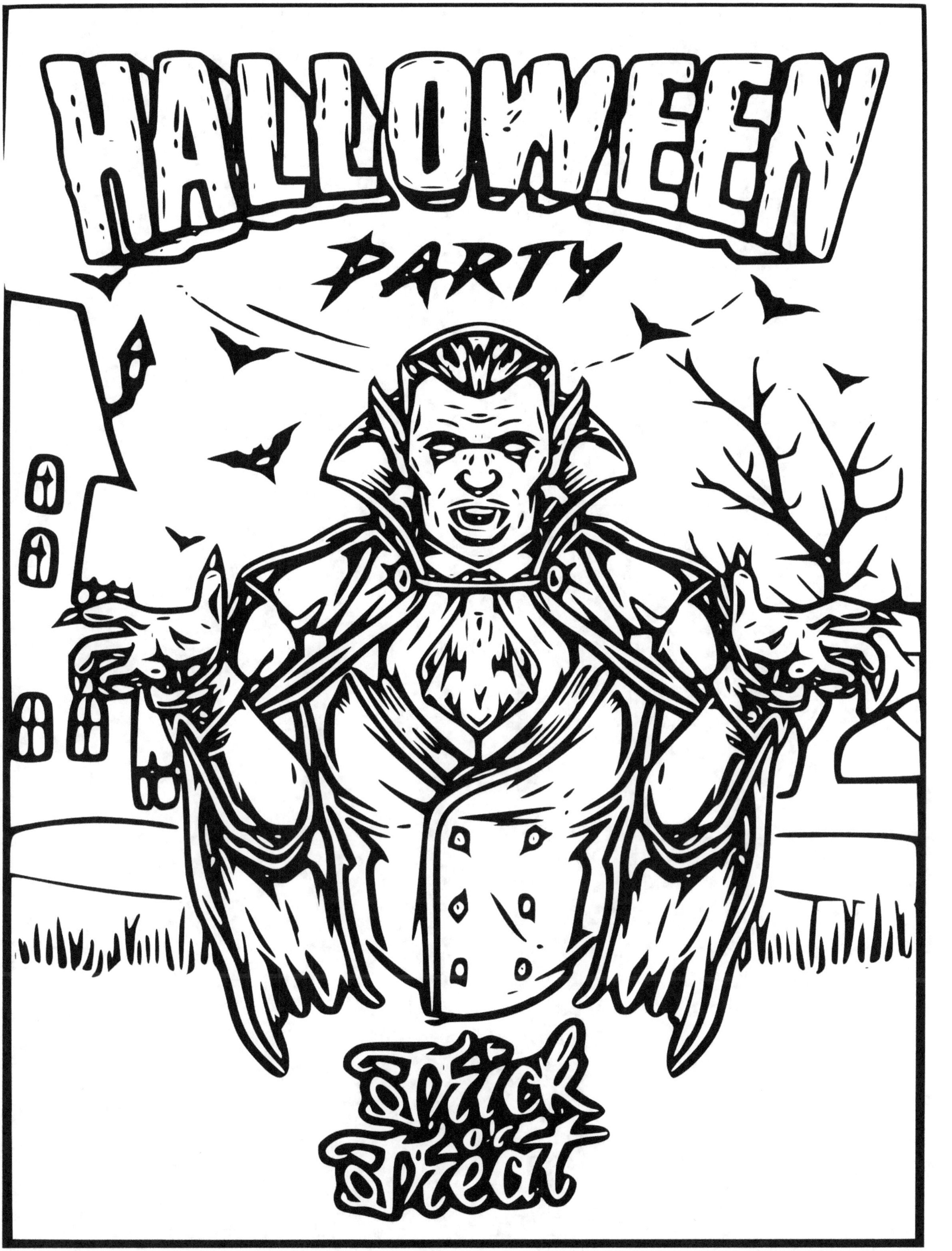
HALLOWEEN
PARTY
Trick
or
Treat

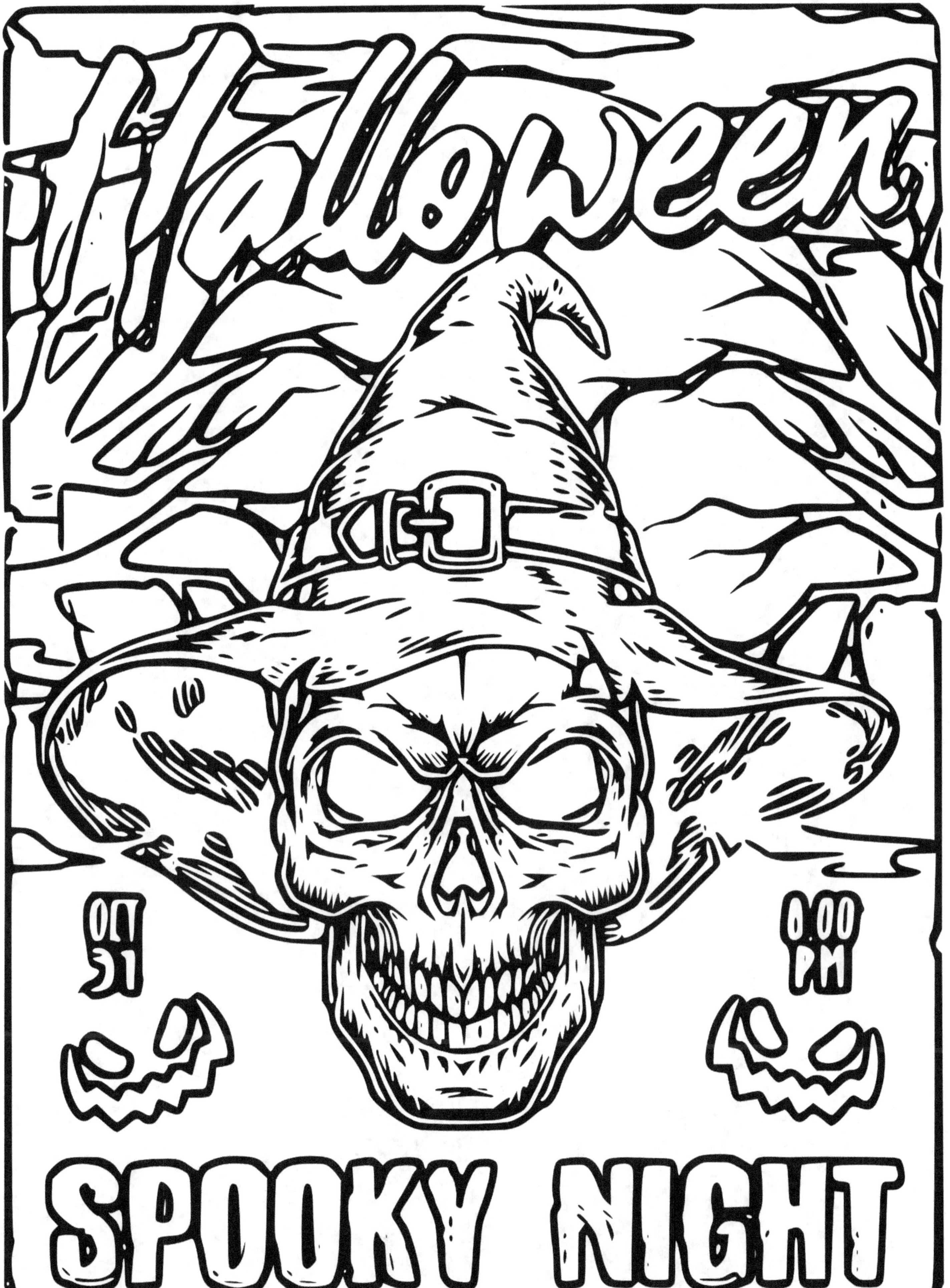
Halloween
0.00
PM
SPOOKY NIGHT

Halloween Party

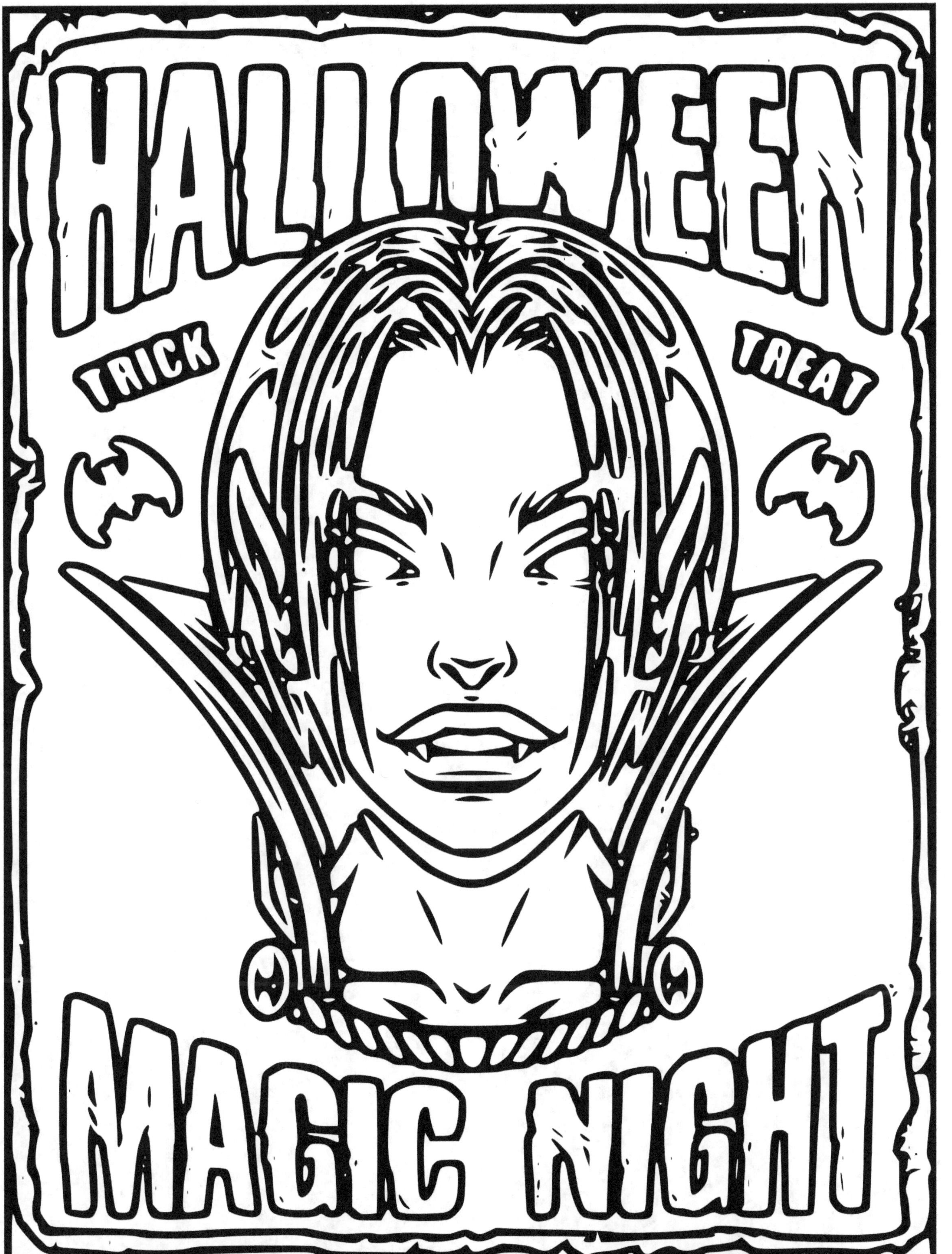
HALLOWEEN
TRICK
TREAT
MAGIC NIGHT

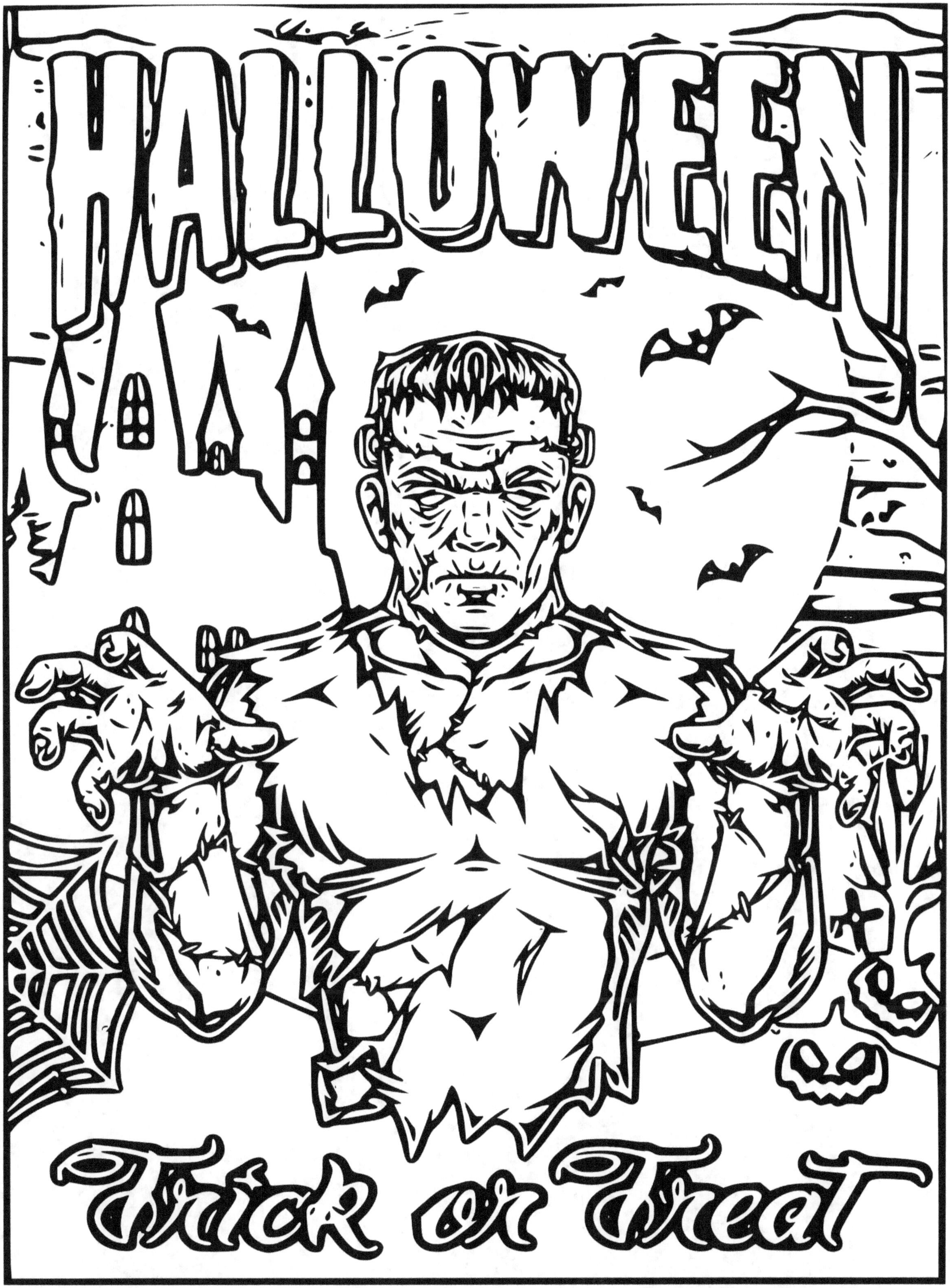
HALLOWEEN
Trick or Treat

Halloween Party

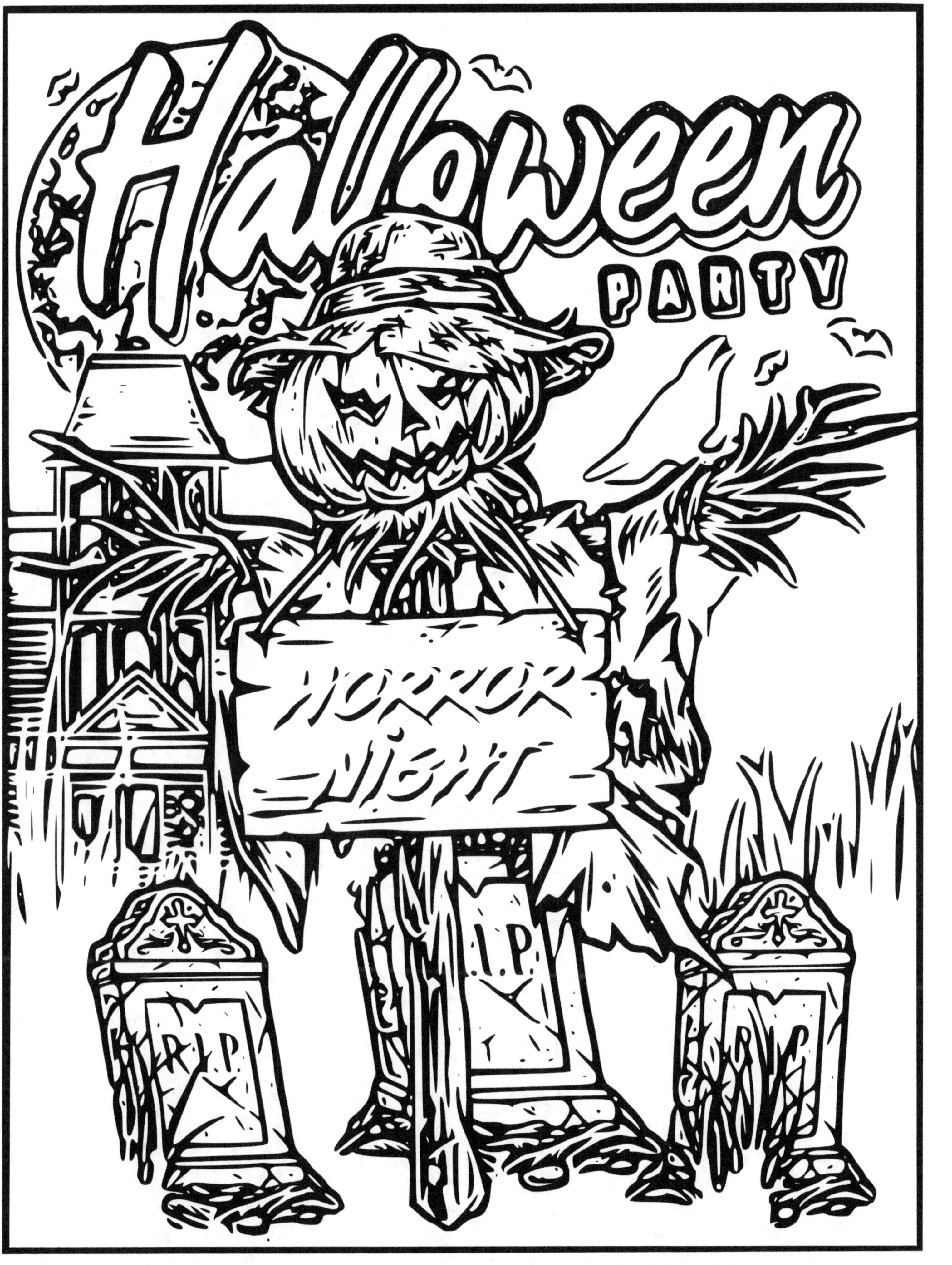
Halloween
PARTY
HORROR NIGHT
R.I.P
I.P
R.I.P

Halloween Party

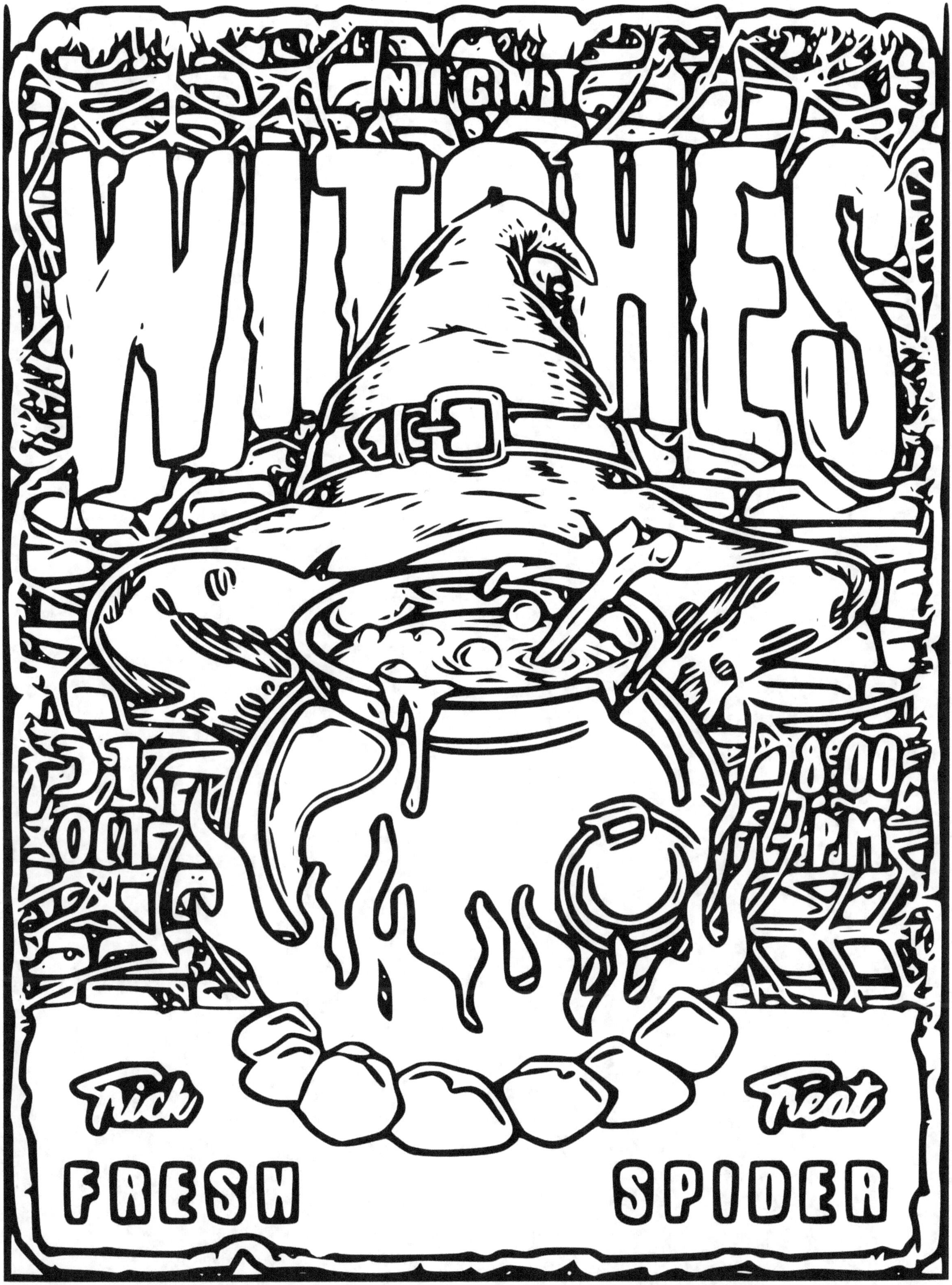
NIGHT
WITCHES
31
OCT
8:00
PM
Trick
Treat
FRESH
SPIDER

Halloween Party

www.ingramcontent.com/pod-product-compliance
Lightning Source LLC
Chambersburg PA
CBHW082150290526
45794CB00008B/3233